T0065469

DIAMONDS
FOR GODLY WIVES

*A Practical Guide for
Young Brides' New Journey*

DALIA GONZALEZ

WESTBOW
P R E S S®
A DIVISION OF THOMAS NELSON
& ZONDERVAN

This book is a work of non-fiction. Unless otherwise noted, the author
and the publisher make no explicit guarantees as to the accuracy of
the information contained in this book and in some cases, names of
people and places have been altered to protect their privacy.

WestBow Press books may be ordered through booksellers or by contacting:

WestBow Press
A Division of Thomas Nelson & Zondervan
1663 Liberty Drive
Bloomington, IN 47403
www.westbowpress.com
844-714-3454

Because of the dynamic nature of the Internet, any web addresses or
links contained in this book may have changed since publication and
may no longer be valid. The views expressed in this work are solely those
of the author and do not necessarily reflect the views of the publisher,
and the publisher hereby disclaims any responsibility for them.

Any people depicted in stock imagery provided by Getty Images are
models, and such images are being used for illustrative purposes only.
Certain stock imagery © Getty Images.

Scripture quotations taken from The Holy Bible, New International
Version® NIV® Copyright © 1973 1978 1984 2011 by Biblica, Inc.
TM. Used by permission. All rights reserved worldwide.

Scripture taken from the Amplified Bible, Copyright © 1954, 1958, 1962,
1964, 1965, 1987 by The Lockman Foundation. Used with permission.

ISBN: 978-1-6642-2378-3 (sc)
ISBN: 978-1-6642-2379-0 (e)

Print information available on the last page.

WestBow Press rev. date: 03/09/2021

CONTENTS

The Housewife

The Mother, Mother-in-law and Grandmother

Recipes

I want to dedicate this book to my mother who went to be with the Lord on August 7, 1998 and who taught me to be the woman, the wife, the mother, the grandmother and the mother-in-law I am today. She was the most incredible woman I have ever met. She was my best friend. From her example, I learned lessons on prayer, love, forgiveness, responsibility, respect and many other values, but most of all she taught me how to be the wife God intended for me to be. My husband and I were married 45 years and though not perfectly, I used every principle on marriage she instilled in me. I love my mother dearly. I also want to dedicate this book to my only daughter Dolly who has been an amazing gift from God to my life, and just for being the wonderful person that she is. She is not only my daughter; she is also my friend and confidant. Through the years, I have tried to pass down to her all the principles from the word of God regarding marriage, diamonds I received from my mother and I know one day, she will also be able to pass on to her children. I love you baby.

THANKS

First of all, I want to thank God for the inspiration of His Holy Spirit as I was putting all this information together. I also want to thank my wonderful husband David, who was my best friend, my helper, the father of my three children, the priest of my home and my first and only love. I don't have enough words to express my gratitude to God for the amazing man he blessed me with. Without him, I don't think I would have been able to finish this project. His understanding, his love, his encouragement, and most of all, his input helped me a great deal. I'm forever grateful to God for the husband He chose for me. We encountered many obstacles on our journey as a married couple, but we conquered them all because of God's forgiveness, love, and grace upon our marriage and our lives. God chose to take him home after a battle with cancer towards the end of the writing of this book. That was the hardest season of my life, and even though my heart was shattered in every way, I thank him for the love he showed me until death parted us and now I rejoice in the fact that he is walking with our King on the streets of gold.

I also want to thank our pastors Joe and Doreen Cotinola for the time spent teaching us and caring for us and our church. Priceless lessons and personal experiences shared which will never be forgotten. They have been right by our side during some of the hardest times of our lives. We love and appreciate them so much. And last but not least our dear friends pastor Chris and Linda Oliva for being our best friends from the moment we met.

ACKNOWLEDGMENTS

I would like to acknowledge two very special young ladies who were the inspiration for this book, Emma (Emmy) Gallardo and Noemi (Mimi) Aguilar. One afternoon, these two young ladies came to spend some time with me. We ate, we prayed, we talked, we laughed and cried together. We had such a wonderful time, but they gave me a passionate desire to help young women like them. They had so many questions and their eagerness to learn more about godly relationship and marriage really motivated me to begin putting things down on paper and under the inspiration of the Holy Spirit I began to write this book. During the time I started writing, neither one of them were even dating. Today they are both very happily married to two wonderful men of God. I pray this book will be a blessing to their marriage as I pray it will become a blessing to many other young brides as they read about "Diamonds for a Godly Wives."

I would also like to acknowledge my two handsome sons David and Jesse, whom I adore and who were used by God as instruments as we learned many lessons on parenthood. They are two very different but wonderful young men. I want to thank God for my awesome daughter-in-law Valerie, whom I admire and respect for the wonderful wife she has been to my son Jesse. She has loved him unconditionally and has been the perfect mother to my granddaughters, Paris and Isela, who captured my heart from birth. And of course I want to acknowledge my first granddaughter Samantha. I want her to know how much I thank God for her and how much I love her as I have seen her endurance through the hard times she has had to face at a young age. Through it all, I admire her for her dedication to her education and for the fine and respectable young lady she turned out to be. I will never forget the memories I built when I had the opportunity to take a break from my writing and repeatedly cook and spend time with her and her high school friends. I fondly remember having so much fun with them during those years.

INTRODUCTION

We live in a society where priorities concerning marriage have been altered and distorted. The world would want you to believe it is OK to behave like some of the wives they portray in movies and soap operas, which is, for the most part, beautiful women in appearance but shallow in her commitment as a wife and a mother. One of the most important things I believe God would want us to do as women of God with a desire to become a wife someday is to set our priorities straight before we say I do. What does God expect of us as a wife, mother and a mother-in-law? **Luke 1:28, "The angel went to her and said, "Greetings, you who are highly favored, the Lord is with you."(NIV)** Mary was chosen by God for the ultimate task of being the mother of Jesus. He saw something in Mary that fit perfectly in the plans He had for mankind when He decided to send His son to this earth to be born of a virgin and later die for our sins. It took a special woman for such a task and that special woman was Mary. In the same way, God has a special plan for each and every woman of God who has chosen to serve and obey God with all of her heart. In the beginning of creation, God's plan for Adam was to bless him with a wife that would love and respect him as the priest of the home. **Genesis 2:18, "The Lord God said, "It is not good for the man to be alone, I will make him a helper who is just right**

for him." (NIV) As Mary was chosen by God to carry in her womb the Son of God, you have also been chosen by God for a special task, to be a wife to that handsome and amazing man of God. Although no one is perfect, it takes a special woman to be an excellent wife. I pray that as you browse through these pages, the Holy Spirit will enlighten you and help you find excellence in this wonderful journey as a wife. As you begin this journey, keep in mind that the road may not always be smooth, but as you begin to use the tools God has given us in His word, though rough, the road will be enjoyable. You will be able to triumph over any difficulty in your endeavor to fulfill God's will for you and your mate as you place your lives in the hands of God.

The moment we say, "I do" is the beginning of a world of responsibilities that could very well be overwhelming for a young couple. If you are not well equipped and prepared for this, "once in a life time" event, soon after the honeymoon, you may find yourself thinking: *"What did I get myself into?"* You will be confronted with many challenging, "do's and don'ts, and crossroad decisions that can become hard to handle at times. Always remember the word of God says: *Ephesians 5:31, "the two will become one flesh" (NIV)* not "the two are one." This means that it will take time for you to become the wife God wants you to be. It does not happen overnight. So in an effort to help you cope with the challenges marriage brings to us women, I would like for you to take a close look at each topic and consider them as diamonds for you to wear daily. You may have already learned some of these principles as you were growing up from your mother, grandmother, aunts, friends or perhaps a mentor as you matured. If so, I pray you will use these as a reminder and begin to apply them as you see necessary. If you have not learned them, I pray it will help you become the wife God wants you to be. In my 45 years of marriage I encountered situations I never thought I would. I learned through them and will share them with others until the day I die.

Through the years my husband and I had what we both believe was "the most wonderful relationship." Most of what I learned came from my wonderful mother, I've also learned by reading books and by following the example of women in the Bible like Sarah who honored her husband to the point of calling him "Master." I've also learned countless lessons from modern day role-models like Julie Arguinzoni, Arline Gonzales, Evelyn (Pogie) Moreno and many others whom I admire for their dedication to God and to their husbands. These women have been married for many years and have succeeded in their endeavor to become wives of excellence. In the next few pages, we will be looking at different tools that have been very helpful in my relationship with God and with my husband. My goal is to encourage every young bride who reads this book to be the wife God wants them to be. I pray you will be able to use these tools early in your marriage as you begin your journey to become "Happily Ever After".

THE WOMAN
OF GOD

I believe that in order to be able to look at your future with great expectations of what your marriage will be, you have to be a *woman after God's own heart, "a woman of God."* No other title better describes what any Christian man would desire for the woman he wants to spend the rest of his life with. A woman who can be described as a "woman of God" has the qualities of a woman of prayer, faith, character, and integrity, among many other wonderful qualities or attributes. Titles may not make a woman, but they define the qualities of a lady. In the next few pages I have made a list of diamonds, each diamond represents a quality. As you read through each diamond, I pray it will help you define the woman of God you really are or would like to be.

1

DIAMOND

A woman of God MUST be a woman of prayer

It was a sunny spring Saturday morning in the month of April. My mother taught me to always clean my room and make my bed as soon as I got up. She said, "If you learn to do these things now, you will always be a good housewife". I had just turned nine years of age and didn't understand too much about life but I knew I had to listen; she was a very strict woman. So, I cleaned my room, made my bed as well as I knew how, got ready, brushed my teeth and went next door to see my aunt. Every Saturday she would save me a little bit of whatever she had made for breakfast. She was what I call my model of a woman of prayer. The Bible was on her kitchen table and she was reading as I ate my breakfast. All of a sudden we heard a loud scream coming from my house. My aunt and I rushed to my house to find a woman holding a knife, threatening to kill my mom. My brother who was in the bedroom had rushed to the living room and was able to save my mom from the hands of my father's mistress. A few days before this happened my father had made a decision to come back home and had rededicated his life to the Lord. He had made the decision to come home to his family after being with his mistress for about 5 years. She was not happy with his decision. The neighbors had called the police. I was too young to fully understand what was going on, and I was very frightened and concerned for my mom. I remember seeing her crying hysterically, so my aunt took me back to her house and told me. "Calm down, your mom is going to be fine, the only thing we can do right now is pray." So we went upstairs to her room and began to pray while my brother, my mom and my dad were dealing with the problem. I could still hear the commotion, the people and the sirens from upstairs as my aunt was praying. Before she finished her prayer, I remember her saying, "Jesus, I thank you for your peace." That was my first experience as a believer in prayer. We must have been in her room for over an hour. I was nervous and crying uncontrollably but my aunt held me in her arms and continued to pray with me until I was able to calm down. By the time we came down, the police had arrested the woman. My mom was crying but there was a peace about her that I couldn't understand. Now I know it was the peace that surpasses all understanding, the peace that only comes from God. I have never been able to forget that time of prayer with my aunt because it was the first time I was able to see prayer turn a massive turmoil into a peaceful atmosphere. It was there where I learned about the power of prayer which is "*diamond number one*" and I have worn that diamond ever since. It is the most important diamond in every situation that needs intervention.

It is in prayer where we learn how to fight against the darts that the enemy constantly throws at our family and marriages. Nothing in this world should be more important to a wife than having a solid relationship with God, falling in love with Him daily. Situations may come and go, some are hard to deal with and some we may think we can handle on our own without praying. Without God's guidance, believe me, no solution for any problem, whether big or small, can be as good as when you place it in the hands of God. When you have a close relationship with our Creator, the biggest turmoil becomes peaceful. ***Philippians 4:6 says, "Do not be anxious about anything but in every situation by prayer and petition, with thanksgiving present your request to God." (NIV)*** In other words, you have nothing to worry about as long as you stay in contact with God in prayer. Prayer is the most important thing in your relationship with your husband. No situation is too big for God to handle. Not only will He handle any situation, but He will give you peace while going through it. ***Philippians 4:7, "and the peace of God which transcends all understanding will guard your hearts and minds in Christ Jesus." (NIV)*** You will have amazing stories to tell your children about the power of prayer in your life, which is the best inheritance you can leave them. Bank accounts, life insurance, properties, businesses or any investment may be important things to leave your children, but the legacy of a woman of prayer is far more important than riches. I grew up in a family with very few resources, but I have memories of my mother praying and crying in the privacy of her room, asking God to meet our needs and I can tell you that every one of those prayers were answered. My father was the love of her life, her first and only love and she adored him. He had an extra marital affair that completely shattered her heart into tiny pieces but she brought my father back home with prayer. As a little girl I would hear my mother many times crying as she was interceding for him before she fell asleep at night and during her prayer time throughout the day. When I would ask her why she was crying, she would always tell me: "I was crying out to God to have mercy on your daddy and bring him back to the Lord and home to us."

I never fully understood what my mother went through until I was faced with the same situation in my own marriage. I also had to experience the pain of being abandoned, rejected and betrayed by the love of my life. It is not something you want to write about but it is something that I believe God allowed me to experience. Even though I wouldn't want to go through it again, I do not regret for a second what God allowed for me to go through because I learned things I wouldn't have known had I not gone through that experience. This experience allowed me to become closer to God than I had ever been, and allowed me to have a much greater understanding of the power of prayer. I know prayer works but to see it in others and experiencing it in your own life is a different story. I became one with the Lord and I knew, at any given time, what He wanted me to do. I learned to listen to His voice and even though I didn't know when my husband was coming back home, I had the assurance that it was going to happen. I was secure in the Lord. Like my mother, I learned to pray and wait on God. For three years I prayed for a miracle, I fought in the spirit. I went to the enemy's camp and took back what he stole from me. God gave me the opportunity to work in the children's department of the Dream Center in Downtown Los Angeles. As I was living and working there, I was able to see my miracle come to pass. We had prayer meetings practically all day long. I would attend prayer meetings in the morning, then at lunch break and sometimes in the evening. Every night for nearly a year, I would go to the roof of our building by myself and talk to God for an hour before I went to bed. Many times I was told not to go to the roof so late at night by myself, it was very dangerous. I never felt alone, I was talking to my heavenly father. It was the most wonderful experience I've ever had. It was like being right there with God, listening to His voice like a child who enjoys the comforting and encouraging words of his or her father. Needless to say, 1999 was the most wonderful year of my life.

So whether you are a "bride to be" or a "newlywed," I encourage you to develop a relationship with God in prayer. I can't stress enough the importance of having a strong relationship with God before you say "I do." I cannot guarantee that you will not face any problems, but if you continue to have a solid prayer life, I can guarantee you a smoother ride on your new journey as a wife. As I mentioned before, I couldn't have imagined, in my wildest dreams, that I would go through the trials I faced in my marriage, but I was well aware of what I needed to do when it happened. I knew how to get a hold of my God and I knew that prayer changes everything. Pray for your husband daily. Pray for God's protection upon his life, and pray that God's keeping power will keep him from failing God. Pray that God will protect his mind from any thoughts that will make him move away from the will of God for his life. Pray that God will cover his ears from hearing any lies of the devil that may seem nice for the moment but will only bring hurt, pain, and confusion in the end. Plead the blood of Jesus on him daily. I am now certain that daily praying and believing in God for my husband has kept him from the hand of Satan upon his life. Many husbands, like mine, were raised in a non-Christian home. If you don't lift him up in prayer daily, who will? Think about it.

Statistics show that money is the number one cause of divorce in America even among Christians. I truly believe it is the lack of prayer. Financial situations need to be lifted to God in prayer and allow Him to be Lord over our lives and remain faithful to Him in our giving. God will always provide if we are faithful to Him. Prayer will move the hand of God on your behalf. *James 5:16, ". . . the prayer of a righteous person is powerful and effective" (NIV)*

2

DIAMOND

A woman of God must be a woman of faith

N ot only do we need to be women of prayer, but we also have to be women who believe in faith that whatever we ask God in prayer it will be given to us. We have to have faith in Him, we have to trust Him blindly and we have to trust in Him even if we cannot see what is ahead. *John 14:1, "Do not let your heart be troubled . . . . . trust also in me." (NIV)* Many times in prayer we say, "I trust you Lord, I believe you can solve any problem," but the minute we finish praying, we continue to worry about that situation. Worry and doubt are the opposite of faith. I realize it is a normal thing for us women to worry about a lot of things because we are very much attached to our feelings and emotions. This makes it hard for us to let go of certain things in our lives. We need to snap out of that concept and begin to believe that God will take care of any situation. I personally have gone through situations where I have said, "I trust you Lord," but I continue to stress about it and hold on to it. But the Lord reminds me of everything He's done for me, then I ask God to give me His peace. The minute I ask for His peace and I begin to worship Him and thank Him for his love for me, the burden is lifted and I am able to see that circumstance from a different point of view. I begin to see that God wants to teach me something and I have to be patient and wait on Him.

God uses every situation we go through. He uses everything negative that happens to us to teach us. You might say, "as a Christian I constantly go through so many things." Those situations should show you how much God loves you. He allows you to go through certain things so that you can grow. He takes time to teach you life lessons with every situation. However, if we don't learn the first time, He keeps trying to get our attention until we are ready to say, "OK God, I'll release this problem to you".

The more God allows you to go through, the more He wants you to learn. So take every problem, every storm, and every disagreement with your spouse as an opportunity to learn and grow. Release it to God and trust Him. He will take care of it. Believe that His promises are true, if He says it is going to happen, believe that it will happen. God is a sovereign God and He has a purpose for everything He allows you to go through.

Let me give you an example. As I mentioned earlier, I went through the same situation my mother went through with my father. Around three months after my husband decided to leave our home, one morning I was praying in my living room. I was battling with all kinds of thoughts, feelings and emotions that were very hard to deal with, things that the enemy kept putting in my mind. I was asking God to speak to me. I needed to hear His voice and I needed confirmation.

That morning, as I was in prayer, I received a phone call

from my sister-in-law who lived in Puerto Rico. She said, *"I just came back from a powerful prayer meeting. The guest speaker spoke to us about the power of prayer. After the meeting I approached her and asked her to pray for my sister-in-law and explained her situation."* The lady said, *"Tell her I will be praying for her. I believe that God has heard her cry, has seen her tears, and He will bring her husband back home."* Those words filled my heart with hope. I knew in my heart that the God I serve was able to answer my prayers. I believed and had faith in God and I knew that He was going to bring my husband home. I didn't know when this would happen, but I expected it to be right away. It was there, that I grew to realize that God is able to work things out for us in his perfect timing. So from that moment on, whenever I felt down or discouraged, I remember that there were others praying for me and my spirit would be lifted.

A year went by, and as I was at work one afternoon, a young man came to the lobby and asked for Dalia Gonzalez, I told him, "that's me". He handed me a big yellow envelope with no name on it and without saying a word, he ran out. I tried to call him, but he took off running so fast, I didn't get a chance to ask him who sent the package. I opened that big mysterious envelope and saw that it contained my divorce papers. The words of that lady came to my mind immediately. I was devastated inside, but I knew, sooner or later, God would bring my husband home. In spite of my pain, I felt peace knowing that God answers prayers. I knew what I was *holding in my hands was just a piece of paper. I knew I just needed to believe and wait on Him"*. I wasn't too happy with the piece of paper, but I made a decision there and then, to continue to believe in the promises in God's word.

Life went on as I kept praying for my husband and waiting on God. Our divorce went through and about a year later, I woke up in the middle of the night and I felt that the Lord was impressing in heart to fast for a few days. As I began my prayer and fasting, I was so encouraged to do so because I thought after the fast, God was preparing something for me. I fasted from Tuesday through Thursday. On Friday, as I was in my office, I received a phone call from a mutual friend of ours who had kept in contact with my husband. He said, "Brace yourself because what I have to tell you may not be what you want to hear." I said, "Is David ok? Please don't tell me something happened to him." He said, "No, David is fine, but he is getting married tomorrow." Again I remembered that God answers prayer in spite of any circumstance. This time, however, I was devastated, but I didn't question God. I knew this was just another piece of paper. I cried out to God, "Please Lord, help me through this, strengthen me, comfort me, and may your will be done. I can't do this on my own, but I have faith in you and I believe in your promises in the Bible.

I made a conscious decision to put my trust in God no matter what. It was not an easy thing to do, when in reality, my husband was no longer my husband, and was now married to someone else. From that point on, I didn't know how to pray for him, but I continued to believe in God and I knew that if I kept my focus on Him, He was going to make the crooked path straight. So I didn't give up and I kept trusting and believing in a God that restores marriages, heals relationships, and mends broken hearts, and He did. If I had given up and not waited on him, like many Christian people had advised me to do, I wouldn't have seen the miracle of God in my marriage.

Proverbs 3:5, "Trust God with all of your heart and lean not on your own understanding." (NIV) Don't go by what you are feeling, or even by what you see. ***1 Cor. 2:5, "... so that your faith might not rest on human wisdom, but on God's power." (NIV)*** Nothing gives God more satisfaction than to see his children relying on Him, trusting in Him, believing in Him. No matter what the circumstances around you look like, God is in control and He will give you the desires of your heart if you only believe in Him. Always remember you are not the only one going through difficult situations. There are many other women of God who have gone before us and have trail-blazed for us. They have been victorious in God and you will be also, if you don't give up. *1 Cor. 16:13, "Be on your guard, stand firm, be courageous and be strong." (NIV)*

3

DIAMOND

A woman of God is a woman of passion for God

Passion is an overwhelming feeling, a consuming zeal, a determination, a purpose-driven emotion. If you want to be a woman who pleases God, you must be a passionate woman. I am not talking about sexual passion; we will talk about that further along. I am talking about a passion to be more like Jesus, a passion for the things of God, a passion for the lost, and a passion for the ministry. This passion does not necessarily have to be full-time ministry. I believe, if you are a Christian who attends church on a regular basis you are in ministry, whether or not you are a leader in the church. Our ministry is to be an example of a woman of God other women would want to follow. A man of God wants and need a wife who is passionate with an eager willingness to serve God in any capacity. A woman who begins and finishes everything she sets her heart out to do. He does not want a woman who is casual about praying, reading the Bible and growing in her walk with God. ***2 Corinthians***

***8:11, "Now finish the work, so that your eager willingness to
do it may be matched by your completion of it. . . . " (NIV)***
In other words, your mate will want you to have a passion for
the things of God because he wants to grow old with you and
finish well. He needs your support in every endeavor he may
undertake to further the Kingdom of God. He wants you both
to finish strong and to do everything for the Lord with love.
***1 Corinthians 16:13-14, "Be on your guard. Stand firm
in the faith. Be courageous. Be strong. And do everything
with love." (NLT)*** He needs a woman who is strong in her
convictions, who is not afraid to follow him in everything he
does for God.

In the early years of our marriage I was not interested in
anything other than to be a wife and a mother. I didn't have
any goals or aspirations for anything other than to have babies,
make sure my husband's needs were met and make sure my
house was clean. Now don't get me wrong, being a housewife
is one of the most important things in a marriage. Doing
practical things like keeping a clean house, doing the laundry,
having dinner ready when he comes home from work, children
are well taken care of and meeting his physical needs. These are
things every married woman has to make sure are done right.
My husband was very happy with me in that aspect, I was
doing all the things that my mother had taught me but he said
I lacked something and it wasn't until later on in our marriage
that I began to realize that what I was lacking was passion.
The passion and determination to have a strong relationship
with God and passion for what my husband wanted to do
for God. I needed to find some kind of connection with my
idea of passion and the passion he had for ministry. I was not
interested on being either a pastor's or a minister's wife. I just
wanted to be a housewife and a mother and I believed I was
good at it. Being the kind of man that he was he would kindly

throw small hints of what he was expecting of me every once in a while, but I was not interested so I didn't pay attention. I wasn't making an effort to understand what was screaming out of his heart.

At that time he was going to Bible school and was very much occupied with his books, homework, term papers etc., as his goal was to be in full-time ministry, whereas I was content with just being a mother and a wife who went to church on Sunday morning. One day we got into a big argument that resulted in us not wanting to continue together. We didn't talk to each other for days, but then we began to miss each other's love and compassion. The Holy Spirit had been speaking to me. I began to realize that just as I had a passion for fulfilling my duties as a mother and housewife, I needed to have a passion for my relationship with God. I was not growing in my spiritual life. I needed to have a balance in my life, so I began to search my heart. I found out that the eagerness I had to provide for my husband's needs, I needed to have for my spiritual needs.

I had known women who were so involved in ministry that they were neglecting their homes, their husbands and their children. I had criticized them not realizing that just as much as they had an imbalance in their life; I also had an imbalance in mine. So I began to pray more and make more time to read the Word of God. Little by little I began to develop a passion for my relationship with God. The passion for ministry began to rise up within me and I wanted to tell the world what I had just learned. My husband began to teach me some of the things he was learning in bible school and I became interested in what he was doing.

That's when I began to understand the plan of God for us as a couple. It wasn't just about going to church on Sunday but it was about having a passionate heart for the things of God while also having a passion for my duties as a wife and a mother. It was not just a desire to go to church; it was an overwhelming desire to hear the message and to worship God. It is not only a desire to see people get saved; it is a determination to minister to people and see them being transformed by the power of God. I was excited about going to church and I began to get our things ready for church the night before. I began to pray that God would give me a strong desire for what He wanted me to do. I prayed for zeal and I began to be determined to do His will for my life.

In order to be passionate, we have to determine in our hearts to be passionate. It begins in the mind, you start thinking about it, and then it is transmitted to your heart. Passion drives you to become more like God. A man of God expects for his wife to be in constant need for more of God. He needs a wife who is in constant communication with God. We need to be women who have an unquenchable thirst for more of Jesus, a woman who wants to please God in every aspect of her life and who is passionate about taking care of her spiritual life.

I suppose you are thinking, "what if my husband is lacking in his spiritual life?" Well, I'm glad you asked. If you stay in prayer, seeking God daily, you will be able to encourage him if and when that happens. As a couple, both of you are one, you belong to one another and the Bible clearly says to encourage each other in the Lord. Encouragement is shown by a positive display of words and actions, there is no need to be pushy. When I came to understand this truth, that was truly the beginning of our relationship.

At that point, we began a triangle with God, the closer we got to God the closer we were to each other. Our arguments diminished and we were able to choose our battles more wisely. I was determined to please God and in doing so, I was pleasing my husband. I was now passionate about prayer, reading the

Bible and attending church every time there was a service. I was passionate about having a close relationship with God.

I encourage you, even now, before you say "I do" (if you are not married yet) to honestly search your heart and see if you have passion for God in your heart. Find out what your mate is passionate about. He may be passionate about sports, a hobby, or perhaps full-time ministry. Whatever his passion is, you need to support him, but make sure to stay passionate together about serving God above everything else. It is the best thing that ever happened to our marriage, even through the struggles we have had to face. My passion to please God has helped me stay strong in the Lord and because of this, we have been able to weather the storms that came our way.

Passion drives you to be all that you can be in the kingdom of God. Passion also drives you to be supportive to your husband in whatever he wants to do for God. Don't give up, don't be a quitter, stay faithful, stand firm in your walk with God and you will see amazing results. I have seen this kind of passion in my pastor's wife Doreen through the years. She has always instilled the same passion for the ministry and the things of God in all of us women in the church. She is a very successful woman of God and I admire her, her example has helped many women achieve success in their own life and ministry myself included.

4

DIAMOND

A woman of God must live a life pleasing to God

Hebrews 12:14, Make every effort to live in peace with everyone and to be holy; without holiness no one will see the Lord. (NIV) When we think of holiness or a holy person, we may think that a holy life would be a dull life. Words like obedience, holiness, sacrifice, and commitment are so unappealing to us. We envision a life spent with boring people doing boring things—no fun at all. I have found that to be so untrue. A holy life is a happy life. The words holiness and happiness go together. King David in the Bible spoke about God's commands and happiness. *Psalms 119:56, "This is how I spend my life; obeying your commandments."*(NLT) If you seek to be a holy person, then you will be a happy person. By holy person, I mean a person who is living to please God, and is happy to obey his commands. So let's try spelling the word holy with a "w," wholly and thinking of it as being wholly committed to God. Giving everything over to Him, letting

Him be the Lord of your life, and letting Him guide your steps. This is the fullest life there is. You will get up in the morning with joy in your heart knowing that God's word and His Spirit will lead you.

None of us can be holy on our own. We try to live by certain regulations, we try to be honest, caring and considerate, but we fall short. So how do we gain access to God's way of holiness? We must come to God and ask Him for His forgiveness, and He makes us holy people. *1 Tim 4:12, "Don't let anyone look down on you because you are young, but set an example for the believers in speech, in conduct, in love, in faith and in purity."* **(NIV)**

A man of God needs a holy woman of God for a wife. Remember the word of God says, **"the two shall become one."** If marriage is a combination of two people, how do you think it would work if one is doing everything in his/her power to live a holy life and the other person is not. Marriage is a triangle with God at the top, and husband and wife on the bottom corners. The closer you both get to God the closer you get to each other. But if one is closer to God, trying to live a life pleasing to Him and the other one is not, the marriage becomes lopsided as you grow apart from each other.

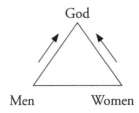

God

Men   Women

Being holy does not mean being perfect. None of us are perfect, but we should strive every day to be more like Him, who is perfect. Problems will come to your marriage and that is inevitable, but when you are living a holy life, God gives you the strength to go through every circumstance with the joy of the Lord in your heart. I found in my walk with God that the only way I could live a holy life, "**wholly**" committed and pleasing to God is by allowing the Holy Spirit to guide me. I learned to rely on God by asking Him every morning to order my steps, and by allowing Him to take over those situations where there was nothing I could do to solve them. There are things I can't do on my own, but with the Holy Spirit on my side, I can trample over snakes and not be harmed. **Luke 10:19, "*I have given you authority to trample on snakes and scorpions and to overcome all the power of the enemy; nothing will harm you*" (NIV)**

There are three very important things that will help you stay holy: 1) prayer, 2) being sensitive to the Holy Spirit, and 3) staying faithful to God in every area of your life. For example, if you work in an office where 99% of your co-workers are not spirit filled, which is usually the case, you will be confronted with many temptations. The devil uses the people we least expect to tempt us with different things. When you are living a holy life and the Spirit of God is in you, you don't have to think about it, you will find it easy to respond immediately to any temptation in a godly manner. You will have no problem responding in a positive way to any temptation. It's not easy to live a life pleasing to God. We live in a world full of corruption and our flesh is weak, but when we make a decision to please God, the Holy Spirit helps us day by day to stay in tune with what God wants us to do. The convicting power of the Holy Spirit raises up a red flag to remind us of the kind of life God wants us to live. *Proverbs 31:30, "Charm is deceptive and beauty is fleeting, but a woman who fears the Lord is to be praised." (NIV)*

A woman who lives a holy life is a woman who fears

God, who delights herself in pleasing God. Not being afraid of God but having a sincere respect and reverence for God. God is pleased with a woman when her priority in life is to be everything God wants her to be. That is the kind of woman any man of God desires to have by his side. When you have the fear of God in your heart, it is easier to resist any temptation of the devil. Your husband will spot you in a crowd of people and say proudly, "that's my wife, my baby, the love of my life." He will feel proud to be your husband and he will trust you in any decision making situation because he knows you are a woman who fears God.

THE WIFE

5

DIAMOND

A wife must be submitted to her husband

Submission versus Authority

B efore we start talking about this subject that has had such a bad status among women in our world and perhaps also in the church, I would like to encourage you to read this with your fiancé or husband. Diamond #5 is for both of you to understand to the fullest and so it is best if you read it together.

> *1 Peter 3:5, "For this is the way the holy women of the past who put their hope in God used to adorn themselves. They submitted themselves to their own husbands." (NIV)*

> *Ephesians 5:25, "Husbands love your wives, just as Christ loved the church and gave himself up for her". (NIV)*

These two scriptures summarize the definition of the word submission in marriage. It is a lot easier for a wife to submit to a man of God who has promised to love her just as Christ loved the church. Christ loved the church enough to die for it. Now husband, are you willing to die for your wife? Well, it doesn't mean you have to literally die for your wife of course, it means you are responsible for her well being. All God requires of you is that you love Him above all things and that you love your wife with all of your heart, mind and soul. Submission for a Christian is defined by the relationship between God the Father and the Son. It cannot be properly understood apart from that. I believe it is unwise for us to uphold the instruction for wives to submit themselves to their husbands as an achievable standard if Christ is not the center of their lives. Without the indwelling power of the Holy Spirit people have neither the discernment nor the power to live out submission and authority in a godly manner.

I have seen many women demonstrate godly submission in the most beautiful ways. One of whom, is my mother. I used to long after her self-assurance and grace. I wished so much I could have been to my husband as she was to my father when I first got married. As I desperately pleaded with God and godly women to teach me, and show me something to help me figure it out, I came to the realization that all the women I looked up to were older. They had done this marriage thing a little longer than I and they were getting good at it. It takes time for a woman to learn submission, but a woman will learn faster if she has a husband who is able to practice godly authority in the home, the way God intended it to be, the way He loved the church and gave his life for it. It also takes a lot of practice. As a man begins to exercise his authority in the home in a godly manner, the woman will be more than happy to practice submission to her husband. Submission and authority work only when they go hand and hand.

We must keep in mind how the media has infiltrated the minds of many married women with ideas that make them believe they don't need to be submitted to their husbands. I have come to the realization that the scripture in **1 Peter 3:5,** was put in the Bible for our benefit and not as a punishment. Some women ask me, "Why is it that the wife is the one that has to be submitted to the husband. Why can't it be the other way around? This is my answer to that question. The husband is the priest of the home, he is the head of the household and God has ordained it that way in his word. *Ephesians 5:22-24, "Wives, submit to your own husbands, as you do to the Lord. For the husband is the head of the wife even as Christ is the head of the church, his body, of which He is the Savior. Now as the church submits to Christ, so also wives should submit <u>in everything</u> to their husbands".(NIV)*

The minute a woman realizes that the husband is the priest of the home and that the authority belongs to him, she begins to see how much he loves and respects her, she will gladly accept his authority. I no longer look at submission as a struggle or a punishment like I when I first got married. To me, it means now I don't have to deal with life's problems and situations on my own. I have a partner whom I can rely on by just submitting myself to his authority as the priest of my home.

The Webster dictionary defines submission as, *"the state of being obedient; the act of accepting the authority of someone else".* As the wife submits to her husband, she is not only being obedient to him, but she is also being obedient to God. In your case as a wife or a wife to be, you have taken or will be taking a vow to be obedient to your husband and in doing so you will be submitting yourself to his authority as the priest of the home.

For some women this is not easy to accept simply because they don't know how and they don't fully understand the rewards of being an obedient and submitted wife to the man she loves.

In the beginning of your marriage it may be a little hard to understand your role as a submissive wife, yet you will do it out of being so in love with this handsome man God has blessed you with. You are in love and willing to do anything he asks, but as time goes by and life becomes a routine, you will find yourself wanting to be independent.

Submission to your husband should not hold you back from being independent. It does not mean that you can't think for yourself or that you can't make decisions on your own. It means accountability; it means that your husband should be aware of everything you do. This way, if he doesn't agree with what you want to do, you are both able to sort things out by talking and reaching a mutual decision. This is what you call submission. I like that my husband knows everything about me and I don't have to lie about anything because he knows that I am submitted to his authority. If I am out with my friends and I am taking a little too long, he knows that if he wants me to come home, I will drop what I am doing and go home. So he doesn't ask me to come home unless it is urgent.. I have no problem being obedient to my husband because he respects my feelings and desires. It is almost like an umbrella of protection I have over me because of his leadership in our home. As long as my husband knows what I do I have no fear of the devil trying to destroy the strong connection we share with each other.

When I think of submission I think of my relationship with God. I realize how my obedience to His Word has protected my relationship with my husband. ***Marriage is beautifully good and beautifully tough, sometimes at the same time. Learning submission is part of that package.***

The husband has the responsibility to love his wife just as Christ loved the church. It is very easy for a woman to submit to her husband if she feels loved, respected and honored. This is why it is most important that this part of the books be read with your mate. It is very important that both know and understand your individual roles in this thing called, "Submission Versus Authority" in the marriage. Just like in any job in which you have to submit yourself to the authority of a boss. It is very easy to do what is expected of you if you are treated with respect. If you are asked to work overtime and you really don't want to, but he then offers to pay you double for your overtime and a bonus at the end of the quarter for your faithfulness to your job, then it becomes easier to respond positively to his request. . In a marriage, if the wife feels loved, respected, and considered by the man she loves it is very easy for her to submit to his authority.

Submission is sometimes learned by example. I learned submission at home. My mother was a submitted woman to God and to my father. Even when he wasn't the best husband she always respected his authority and she expected the same respect from us children to our father. As a newlywed, I struggled and struggled with what submission looked like in my marriage. I am a stubborn, independent person and even though I had seen my mother's submissive spirit, submission was not in my nature. I was the only daughter and youngest child. My father spoiled me to death so it was easy to submit to him. But when I realized I needed to submit to my husband's authority it was a different story. Why? Because my husband was not my daddy. I had to learn to submit to the authority of my husband the hard way, and I had to learn it not just for my own benefit but also for the sake of our children who were watching every step I took. I knew what I needed to do but I was too stubborn to give in to my husband's authority.

I want to emphasize the fact that if we want our offspring to learn about submission and authority, it must begin at home between mom and dad. Submitting to authority in the home will have an impact throughout their lives. Notice I said my mother was submitted to God, then to my father. If we learn to submit ourselves to the will and direction of our heavenly father it will become easier to fall under the submission to our husbands. Submission is not a bad word for a woman if she understands the effects and rewards of her obedience to God. Authority in a man will not overpower him with pride if he understands the effects and rewards it has in his marriage as he loves and respects his wife just as Christ loved the church.

EXAMPLE OF A NON-SUBMISSIVE WIFE

An example of an area in which you have to be totally submitted to is your husband's direction. Let us compare submission versus authority. It is easy for some women to submit to their husbands in some areas but not in others. When it comes to finances some woman have a very hard time submitting to their authority. I understand that some women are better at managing the finances of the home than men. But as I mentioned before money, is the #1 cause of quarrels in a marriage. *1 Timothy 6:10, "For the love of money is a root of all kinds of evil. Some people, eager for money, have wandered from the faith and pierced themselves with many griefs.* **(NIV)** It is because some couples don't think it is important to budget their finances together. I don't need to earn an income to be independent; I can be free with or without a personal income. Some women, because of financial hardship in the home, have been obligated to join their husbands in the work force and I understand that, but many women have the wrong idea of what a married working woman must be. Their motives have proven to go entirely against what God intended for a marriage to be. Before we go any further, let me tell you, I am not against women working.

I worked from the time my youngest child entered Kindergarten until all three of our children were married and gone. My husband said, "it's time for you to stay home, we can live off my income only." I was as happy to finally stay home as I was when I first started working. I understand there might be a need for two incomes in a household. Most American families must have two incomes to be able to survive. But that does not make a woman independent nor does it give her the right to spend her money as she pleases. There has to be a balance. My husband and I have never had two bank accounts. We have always put both of our paychecks together, and we made our budget together, counting on both of our incomes.

A few years back a sister came to me and said, "Sister Dalia, I just wanted to give you a praise report. Remember when I asked you to pray for me because I needed a job desperately so I could help my husband with our household bills? Well, I got the job and I am so excited. I already met some of the other girls in the office. They invited me to lunch and they made me feel so welcome to their little group. It was really God that provided this job for me because I had no experience and I want to thank you for praying for me."

She wouldn't stop talking and wouldn't let me say a word. She continued saying, "Remember how I was stressed out when my husband was on disability? We were barely making it and we got behind in all of our bills. Now he's back to work and I don't mind helping with our household bills, in fact I'm excited because as long as I help a little with some of the bills my husband doesn't have to know how much I make or what I do with the rest of my money. "I go to work just like him, so obviously I no longer have to be submitted to his authority concerning finances like I was when he was the only one working." She went on and on telling me everything she didn't have to do now that she had become, financially independent. I let her talk and I listened for a while. I guess she needed to let out all her excitement.

After a while I said, "Sister, have you and your husband talked about all this you are telling me?"

She said: "Oh no, I haven't, but when my friends at work took me to lunch, I was listening to them talking about how they don't let their husbands know how much they make, so they won't be questioned about every penny they spend. One of them was talking about the $300.00 purse she had just purchased. Another one was saying she spent $200.00 on a new line of makeup she saw. My other co-worker bought 5 pairs of high heels that were on sale and she only paid $400.00. I got so excited about all their comments and I started thinking about all the things I could do with my money. What do you think, Sister Dalia? Is that biblical?"

I said, "let me ask you again before I answer your question. Have you talked to your husband about the things you are telling me? Have you planned for your future now that there's more income coming into your home?

She said: "No, by the way I just got my first credit card. Isn't that exciting?

I said, "Sister, you really need to think about everything you are telling me. I am not against women working, but when you leave your husband out of any area of your life, that is not biblical. It is like being dishonest with your husband about something that really concerns both of you. To top it all off, when you were making all those plans to buy this and that and the other, did you remember to honor God first with 10% of your income?

To that she answered, "No, I thought the tithe would come from his income since he is the priest of the home." In my mind I thought, Oh my God please help me with this one, she is not going to like what I am about to tell her.

I said, "let me tell you, the moment you said I do, you began a new chapter in your life. No longer are you one but as the bible says, "the two shall become one." This means every important decision in the home must be made between both husband and wife. With this, I don't mean that you can't go to the market and decide whether to buy chicken or beef for dinner without consulting with your husband. There are things you can do without asking him. But when it comes to finances and how to plan for the future of your family, it is of outmost importance to sit together and decide what needs to be done, otherwise your marriage won't last."

She answered, "Sister Dalia, you mean to tell me I work hard for my money, but I can't spend it as I please?"

"Yes, that is exactly what I mean."

Her face changed from being excited to being depressed. I told her, "it's really not as bad as you think. In fact you will feel more independent to do what you want with your money after you have paid your tithe and all your bills in the home and have money left to buy anything you want as long as your husband knows about it.

She said, "Sister Dalia I don't know if I can do that, you don't know my husband, he will never let me buy anything I want."

"Well there must be a reason why, maybe there are some bills that are more important than a new line of make-up, don't you think? I love new and expensive purses and I love top of the line make-up and shoes and all the things that women love, but there is a time and a place for everything." She wasn't too happy but she promised me she was going to sit and talk to her husband about our conversation.

My point is just as we have learned to submit our will to the will and purpose of God, we should also learn how to submit ourselves to the authority and leadership of our husbands. Yes, I understand some men are not as good as women when it comes to finances but it is very important that you sit with him and discuss what is essential to be paid and how much each of you have to spend on what you want and need after the tithe and bills are paid.

It is also very important to save for the future. Having a savings account is the wisest thing any couple can do. There are many other things I could tell you that would help you learn how to be submissive wife but, every marriage has its unique way of dealing with submission and authority. Therefore you need to sit with your husband and discuss ways in which you can submit to him and how he can exercise his authority in the home.

6

DIAMOND

A wife must be her husband's best friend

Song of Songs 5:16, "His mouth is sweetness itself; he is altogether lovely. This is my beloved, this is my friend. . . " (NIV)

The word friend is defined in the dictionary as, "a person attached to another person by feelings of affection or personal regards." Your husband needs a companion, a confidant, a trustworthy person, and a good listener, not a critical listener. In other words, he needs a friend. You can only find these qualities in a good friend.

When you were growing up you became friends with the girl who showed you affection and respect in the simplest way. She would listen to you without criticizing you. You enjoy doing fun things together and even shared secrets. Then you became an adult, met your husband and became attached to him when he showed you affection and respect. You began to find things you had in common and felt comfortable talking to him about different things. As the relationship became more serious, you were able to talk to him about everything to the point where you could talk for hours and still felt like you could to talk to him for another four hours. Even when he didn't agree with what you were saying, you felt comfortable talking to him. Well, he needs to feel the same way with you all the time. A man needs a woman who will support him even when she doesn't agree with him. A friend will do just that.

Let me explain this a little further. On this journey we call marriage, you will find yourself many times not thinking the same way your mate thinks. In other words, you have different points of view, and that is called disagreeing. This is not a negative point in your relationship. It is human to be and think different than that person you love so much. It is perfectly all right to disagree, what is not right is when you take the disagreement to another level. I call that selfishness. Everything is about you, I am right, you are wrong; it's your fault, not mine. Your husband is going to need someone who, in spite of your differences or different points of view, he feels respected by his wife.

When a friend comes to you with an idea of something she wants to do, even if you don't agree, what do you say to her? Do you tell her, "I don't think you should do that but if you think it's going to work for you then go for it?" Or do you tell her, "I don't think you should do that and if you do it, don't talk to me again? Which answer would you give her? If you love and respect your friend, you give her your opinion and let her make her decision, even if you think it is a mistake. In a marriage you have to go a little further than that. It's not good for you to tell your husband that you don't like his idea and that is final. You need to talk about whatever it is that he wants to do and discuss the pros and cons together. Then you need to pray and ask God to show both what would be the best way to handle that specific situation. God will always give you the right counsel. If, after doing that, you still feel he is doing the wrong thing, then there are two things you can do. You can stand your ground and be upset at him for weeks which will make things worst or you can tell him that even though you don't agree with his decision, you trust he is doing the right thing. If you leave it in God's hands and he is wrong, God will speak to his heart and if you are wrong, God will speak to your heart. If you both continue to be stubborn and you both can't agree, then it is time to bring in a third party. A counselor, pastor, or a mutual friend, whom you both trust and respect and who has been married for a long time, can give you godly advice.

We as women need a friend that will listen without making us feel we are always wrong. I'm sure you have had friends who are negative about everything and friends who are positive. Which friend do you trust with your personal life issues, the negative friend or the positive friend? I'm sure your answer would be the positive friend. You know she would understand what you are going through and would encourage you with positive advice. Well, it is the same with our husbands. They need a wife who will be a friend, who will understand and give them words of encouragement, rather than some cutting, disappointing or discouraging words when they have a problem or they just need a friend to share things they can't share with just anyone. Would you want to be the friend he trusts, or would you rather him go to someone else to share his feelings? Think about it before you answer that question. If you are one of those people who do not have patience to sit and listen to anyone talk about their problems, you may be in big trouble if you can't listen to your own husband. He might end up finding someone else who will listen. If you are ok with that you might need to pray that the other person he finds is a male friend, a brother in the Lord, a pastor or a mentor. Sometimes we all need to have a heart to heart talk with someone we really trust. But be careful because it can be a woman, "very dangerous." Perhaps if you are an understanding woman of God, he wants you to be, he will not feel the need to go to anyone else to share his personal feelings.

I was married to my best friend and sad to say, it wasn't always like that. I didn't have the patience to sit and listen to my husband's issues and problems. I thought I was a good wife, but I realized when my husband and I were separated that he needed someone who would listen and encourage him. When he left, I tended to blame myself for everything that had happened but the Lord spoke to me and showed me that I was not to be blamed for anything he did but I needed to learn a few things. One of them was to be a good listener and pay attention to my husband's feelings. To be a listener when he wanted to talk, and pay attention to whatever his heart was saying. In other words, I needed to become his friend. Now we are best friends, we can both talk to each other about everything with no reservations. I have learned to listen and encourage him even when I don't agree. If I don't agree I say this, "Babe, I don't understand why you are feeling that way or I don't agree with what you are wanting to do but, I'm going to pray about it and ask God to help you make the right decision. If I am wrong, I'm sure God will reveal it to my heart." Those words mean more to him than negative, impulsive, wanting to always be right, kind of statements. If your husband can find a friend in you, I assure you, you will always have a friend in him. Don't let someone else be his best friend. He is your husband, the love of your life and you should be his best friend.

7

DIAMOND

A wife must be a loving wife

1 Corinthians 13: 4-8, "Love is patient, love is kind, it does not envy, it does not boast, it is not proud, it does not dishonor others, it is not self seeking, it is not easily angered, it keeps no record of wrongs. Love does not delight in evil but rejoices with the truth, always hopes, always persevere. Love never fails. . . .(NIV)

In a nut shell this scripture describes what God expects of us. Let's look at this scripture as if He was talking face to face to us. He wants you to be **patient**, even when you think you have run out of patience. **Kind**, when kind words or actions don't come to mind. **Not envious**, when you see your husband succeeding in any area of his life, or when you see other women having things you can't have. **Not boastful**, when speaking about yourself. **Not selfish**, putting yourself above him, discrediting his name, especially in front of others.

Not angry about every mistake he makes. **Not remembering** during every argument or disagreement, something he did months or years ago. **Never lying** but always keeping the truth as a way of life, always hoping for the best and never giving up on him. If you love him you will try your best not to ever fail him. That is the way God wants you to love him.

LOVE UNCONDITIONALLY

I am sure you are reading this book because you are completely head over hills, madly in love with the man God blessed you with. Otherwise, you wouldn't be interested in learning anything about how to please him. The best way you can assure him that he made the right decision when he ask you to marry him, is by showing him your unconditional love and respect. Show him that you love him in spite of his faults, idiosyncrasies, habits, routines, behavior, character, personality, and temperament. Show him that no matter what, you will be true to the vow you made before God to love him, comfort him, honor him, and keep him, for richer, for poorer, in sickness and in health and forsaking all others keeping yourself **only** unto him as long as you both shall live.

Marriage is forever, it's not something you can start today with the idea that if it doesn't go as you as expected you can end it tomorrow. The love you promised him at the altar is forever. The Bible says what God put together, let no man separate. A husband needs to feel loved and the way he feels loved is through your admiration for him. You have to let him know you admire him above any other man in this world. In public; he needs to feel that you are on his side, to defend him above anyone else. Do you want to feel that you are number one in his life? Well, he needs to feel the same.

USE THE RIGHT WORDS

Two words should not exist in a marriage disagreement, never and always. I have seen these two words thrown freely back-and-forth in marriage counseling sessions: You never throw the trash out, you're always leaving your clothes all over the place, you never buy me flowers, you are always watching TV. If you think about it, they are all lies. It is not true that he never throws the trash, or he is always watching TV. I'm sure there are times when he would rather do fun things with you, and there are times when he helps around the house. Many women have the habit of using negative things they do in an argument that has nothing to do with throwing the trash or watching too much TV, etc.. All you are doing is putting him down, expecting a reaction from him. You will never be able to get a positive reaction from a man when you are using negative terms about what he does. If you want a positive reaction from him, sit and have a calm conversation with him, at a moment when he is not watching TV or resting after a hard day at work, when he can give you his full attention. I guarantee that you will get more out of that conversation than with a conversation during a disagreement. Remember that he can also say things like: you never clean this house or you are always on the phone, etc. We show love when the biggest mistakes are handled in a positive way, not with harsh words or negative statements. It is very important that you think before you speak and choose your words wisely. ***Proverbs 18:21, "The tongue has the power of life and death and those who love it will eat its fruit.* (NIV)**

"Ever After," is the title of one of my favorite movies, and I have watched it over and over. It is really a Cinderella story, and after she had gone through all the abuse and harsh words spoken to her by her step mother, she finally marries the Prince. The King, which is now her father in law, asked her, "what do you want us to do to your stepmother?" Cinderella says, "I just want you to have the same respect she has always bestowed upon me." The stepmother tried to defend herself when she was interrupted by the Queen, which is now Cinderella's mother in law, and she says to her, "***Choose your words wisely madam, for they may be your last.***" I chuckle every time I see how this woman made a fool of herself in front of the King and Queen and a room full of city officials. She finally ends up in the laundry department of the castle.

This brings me back to a very dark time in my life when I said some very harsh words to my husband. Those words were the last ones I said to him before he left to be with another woman and I was left alone with a bag full of guilt and shame. We must be wise with the words and the tone of voice we use to talk to our husbands because one day they may be our last. God has a way of showing us things, sometimes, that can be devastating for us. But if we yield our lives to his will and purpose it will turn our lives around for the best. God did restore our marriage but it was after three distressing years and a long list of lessons learned. My suggestion to you regarding this is 1) Never use harsh words when disagreeing about any issue. But if you do, 2) Do not let him walk out the door before taking time to discuss the issue in a civil manner because worse scenario, you may never see him alive again, or he may find someone that will treat him with more respect than you and you will be left alone with a bag full of guilt and shame. Even if it wasn't your fault, the enemy will make you feel like it was. **Once words leave your mouth they can never be taken back. If you love your husband you will respect him, if you respect him he will show his love.**

> ***Proverbs 15:1, "A gentle answer turns away wrath but a harsh word stirs up anger" (NIV)***

8

DIAMOND

A wife must have a forgiving heart

L ove is followed by forgiveness. If you love you will be able to forgive. The Bible says we ought to forgive those who sin against us over and over and over. *Luke 17:4, "Even if they sin against you seven times in a day and seven times come back to you saying "I repent" you MUST forgive them. (NIV)* How many times have you needed for someone to forgive you, and you have felt their forgiveness? God himself forgave all of our sins and will continue to forgive us and he forgives us because he loves us. Your husband is not a perfect man and I can assure you that there are going to be times when you are going to feel hurt with things he will say or do to you. You are going to need his forgiveness. Forgiving is not easy, it takes love to forgive. Forgiveness must come from the heart. It can't be just saying, I forgive you, and continue not to talk to him or continue with an attitude. We women are good at that. If you don't feel you have forgiven him, it's best you don't say you have. If that is the case, it is time to hit your prayer closet again. Begin to ask God to help you understand what took place and find forgiveness in your heart for your husband. You will never forget what he did to you but you will be able to forgive and go forward. Keep in mind, I am not telling you to do something I haven't done myself. Some things are easier to forgive than others. I forgave my husband's infidelity. I pray you never have to experience what I had to endure. It was the hardest thing I had ever done but I was able to forgive him because I loved him. I had to look beyond his infidelity, as ugly as it was, and try to look at it as something God allowed in our lives to teach us, mold us and prepare us for the relationship we have now. Notice, I said God allowed, he did not make it happen. When something like infidelity happens, there are different levels you go through: feeling hurt, mad, feeling sorry for yourself, having an, I don't care attitude, to mention a few. There was one level that really helped me through that ugly ordeal and that was "releasing."

Releasing came to me the minute I said to myself I forgive him. I said to God, "I release my husband to you, I release my anger, my hurt, and my unforgiving heart to you Lord, do with me as you please." The moment I said those words the spirit of God came like a flood and surrounded me. I felt like a burden had been lifted from my shoulders. I felt like a brand new person, I felt relieved. Yes, I know this was an extreme situation, but what I'm trying to say is that there is no sin big or small that can't be forgiven.

There are three things I advise you to do when you feel your husband has hurt you in any way, release, reflect and reunite:

1. **Release** it to God in prayer.
   Releasing issues to God is one of the most important things we can do if we want to forgive from the heart.

Asking God will help you deal with the issue as he shows you what you need to do and how to do it.

2. **Reflect** on what happened.

   Think about the events prior to the argument. Remember it takes two to tango. Think about what could have made him react the way he did. Think about what you could have said or done differently.

3. **Reunite** with your husband.

   Try to look at the issue from his point of view. Make sure you resolve the problem before you go to bed that night, before your anger begins to damage your heart. Always remember hurt can turn into hate, hate turns into bitterness and bitterness will damage your heart, sometimes permanently. So I encourage you before your hurt feelings go any further, deal with the problem. There is no problem too big for God to handle. Lift that burden to God in prayer and make time to speak to your husband ASAP. Making up after a time of forgiveness is the best part about being married and that takes us to our next diamond.

9

DIAMOND

A wife must be her husband's lover

A man and a woman's relationship must not be built on a sexual foundation, but rather on a spiritual foundation. The world's mentality is based on living together before marriage. After many years, if they feel they get along fine then they make plans to get married. Other couples move in together out of love for each other but legalizing their union with a marriage ceremony becomes less important as time goes by. In Christianity, we believe that if a couple can maintain a relationship built on a spiritual foundation without sexual intimacy before marriage, then they will definitely have God's blessings on their marriage. Why? Because that is the way God intended marriage to be. Love making is the most beautiful thing God created between a man and a woman. It is a critically essential part of any marital relationship, but marital problems have grown in our culture because people assume that intimacy will sustain a relationship. In order for any Christian couple to have amazing sexual intimacy, there must be spiritual intimacy.

Spiritual intimacy happens when both husband and wife surrender their lives and their relationship to the Lord. You grow together spiritually when you live out your marriage relationship according to God's ways, and your aim is to please him in all things. As I mentioned in Diamond #4, we must aspire to live a holy life.

Spiritual intimacy is not available to everyone. It is an ingredient that is available only to those who have a personal relationship with God through Jesus Christ and who live to please him. When you join your life with a man in a Christian marriage, you have the wonderful privilege of seeking spiritual intimacy in your marriage. When a married couple is experiencing spiritual growth in their vertical relationship, their horizontal relationship comes together as well.

Spiritual growth is a duty as a Christian for both husband and wife. Spiritual intimacy happens when you experience God together and share what you have learned. It is possible that you don't realize the power that spiritual intimacy can have on your relationship. ***Emotional and physical attraction is what drew you together, but spiritual connection is what will keep you together.***

Let's look at 7 of the benefits of spiritual intimacy in a marriage

1. It gives you the power to celebrate love.
2. It allows you to connect with each other at the deepest level.
3. It links you with God's purposes and plans for you as a couple.
4. It allows you to bless each other with God's love.
5. It brings your deepest desires into agreement.

6. It opens the door to the highest levels of communication.
7. It gives your marriage the power to survive.

The most important thing in your marriage is having a relationship with God. So as we mentioned before, praying together and individually, reading and studying the word of God together, being accountable to each other by sharing what you learn, and being willing to receive spiritual encouragement as well as correction from each other, will definitely help you grow spiritually as a couple. Continue to work daily towards spiritual intimacy. The greatest gift you can give each other is a lifelong commitment to spiritual growth. But if you lack spiritual intimacy you may find yourself encountering conflicts in many other areas. It doesn't mean that if for any reason, you go to bed one night and you both feel the desire to be intimate but you haven't prayed or read the bible you need to stop and pray. No, I am not saying that at all. But things will go much better once you are engaging in the sexual part of your relationship when you have taken time to honor God. I encourage you to set a time to pray and seek God.

PRACTICAL TIPS FOR INTIMACY

1. ***Always make sure you look beautiful and you smell pretty for him***. The moment you say I do is the time to get rid of all flannel pajamas and old t-shirts you used to wear when you were single. Now you have a husband who desires to see his wife beautiful every night. Remember men get excited by what they see. Sexy lingerie is very appealing to him and is very important in love making. If you don't have anything sexy or cute to wear that night, which is hard to believe, since I know your friends showered you

with plenty of cute stuff at your wedding shower, it is best not to wear anything, (LOL, funny but true). Believe me, he will enjoy that better than an expensive piece of garment. Women get excited by what they feel; the caressing, the touch, the kissing, the embrace, and by the sweet words she hears from her man but *men get excited by what they see.* You want to keep that excitement going in your bedroom all through your marriage. That excitement will keep the enemy away from your husband's mind and intimacy in your marriage. Whether intimacy happens or not, allow him to see and smell a beautiful and loving wife next to him every night. My mother always told me before I got married, *"always make sure you take a shower before bed time, you never know what can happen in the middle of the night."* I always thought she told me that in case I got sick in the middle of the night and had to be taken to the hospital, I would be clean. Well after I got married she told me, "the reason *I taught you to bathe before bed time is because I wanted you to make a habit of it and when you got married you would always be ready for your husband at night."* I just passed on my mother's little secret to you. Needless to say, intimacy doesn't always happen at night or always in bed. It can happen any time of the day and anywhere in the house and when that happens, of course you are not going to stop the flow to go get clean. There are also going to be moments where you will enjoy doing spontaneous things in the privacy of your home and it is perfectly alright to enjoy those moments without feeling guilty.

2. **Make sure the environment in your room is pleasant**. A good idea is to keep the room clean at all times, with clean and fresh sheets and pillowcases. Soft scented candle lights in your room will always bring a soothing sense of

romance and will be very inviting to your husband. An occasional candle light dinner is very appetizing. If he is tired from working all day, encourage him to rest for a while. In the meantime, prepare him a simple succulent meal and take it to him in bed or prepare an elegant place at the dinner table for two. After the meal you can be the dessert, the possibilities are endless. If the room is clean and picked up and the sheets are clean and fresh, you can make him feel as if he is in an elegant five-star hotel room for the night.

3. **Never tell him "NO"** unless for health reasons or spiritual separation, you would rather not be intimate with him at that moment. But in that case, explain the reason why and make sure he understands. Do not allow him to feel rejected without an explanation. God made men and women's bodies to function in very different ways. Men have unique needs which must be fulfilled more often than our needs. Their sex drive is usually stronger than ours. Of course there are exceptions; some women have a very high volume of hormones in their bodies which allow them to have a stronger sex drive than most women. When those needs arise in a man, a release of body fluids (sperm) must take place. If you continue to reject him or avoid intimacy with him, those fluids will accumulate causing emotional frustration, moodiness, and consequently other forms of release may take place, like what they call "wet dreams" or masturbation, which is not a good practice especially for a married man. As godly wives we have been called to fulfill those physical needs in our husband's bodies. Fulfilling his needs should not be a duty. It should be an enjoyable experience and a wonderful time for both of you. Remember that intimacy starts in the mind, so begin to prepare yourself mentally as soon as you see the moment

approaching. To help you with this, I suggest you begin to reminisce on the good times you have had together. Some women will say I don't know what a climax is. Sexual climax is the ultimate feeling any woman can experience in intimacy but I suggest you talk to your mate and read Christian books that give you a better explanation. If you feel embarrassed talking to your husband about that, talk to a close friend or someone you can trust. Sometimes it takes the women a little longer to get prepared for that moment and many times foreplay with your husband will help you reach that exciting point faster. This process will help you view intimacy as something exciting, an enjoyable moment with your husband rather than a duty or something you are forced to do. If, after trying all these tips, you continue not enjoying your intimate time with your husband, I suggest you both seek professional help like your doctor, your pastors, or the marriage counselors in your church. Now, by all means do not get in the habit of using that old phrase many women love to use, "*Not tonight, I have a headache.*" Believe me, if you have a headache you will find sexual intimacy the best cure for it.

4. **There are do's and dont's in intimacy:** There is a book called, "The Art of Love Making" and I recommend you read it. I would like for you to consider the fact that God desires for you to live a pure life before him. The scripture below talks about the "*marriage bed being undefiled,*" which means to honor the marriage bed. Everything done in the privacy of your bedroom should be pleasing to God.

> **Hebrews 13:4, (AMP)** "*Marriage should be honored by all and the marriage bed kept pure, for God will judge the adulterer and all sexually immoral.*"

DO'S AND DON'T'S OF INTIMACY:

Pornography is one of the reasons why some marriages have ended up in divorce. Men or women who have allowed themselves to be driven to pornography may likely have turned off their spouses at a time of intimacy. Pornography is lusting over another person other than your spouse. Lust is a sin and eventually will destroy a marriage. ***1 John 2:16, "For everything in the world-the lust of the flesh, the lust of the eyes, and the pride of life-comes <u>not</u> from the Father but from the world"*** **(NIV)**

Sodomy (anal or oral copulation with a member of the opposite sex) Is also a sin and some couples believe that whatever you do in the intimacy of your room is permissible because it is between you and your spouse. But not everything is permissible. The word of God speaks very specifically about certain issues. Always make time to discuss with your husband your likes and dislikes about your intimacy. If you keep God in the center of your relationship, you will not desire to do things that are not pleasing to God. Keeping your love-making godly will allow you to enjoy each other on a deeper level. Communication, as you know, is the most important tool in a marriage. Talk to him and let him know how you feel about things you are not comfortable doing.

Fantasizing is visualizing or letting your imagination run wild about another person or entertaining the thought of something you have seen or perhaps done with someone other than your mate. It is like inviting a third person into your bedroom. Once that happens, it is very difficult to take that other person out of intimacy with your mate.

Masturbation is self-stimulation of genitals, especially geared towards orgasm. it is sexual self-gratification. The moment you said, "I do," your body began to belong to your husband according to the Word of God.

> ***1 Corinthians 7:4, "The wife does not have authority over her own body, but yields it to her husband. In the same way, the husband does not have authority over his own body but yields it to his wife" (NIV)***

Let me mention a few things that can enhance intimacy and make it more enjoyable for both of you.

Different Positions ~ A women came to me one day and said, " is it wrong to make love in a different position other than the normal way?" I responded by saying, "What is the usual way? As far as I know there is no book or manual that says intimacy or love making is to be done in a certain way or position. In fact, finding different positions, or a different place to make love, brings a sense of excitement to the act of sex. So no, it's not wrong to allow yourself to have fun during intimacy with your husband as long it's kept holy.

Play Games ~ Playing games is a wonderful way to bring versatility to intimacy with your mate. Games like, "playing hard to get," or you can be creative with your sexy body just to please him.

10
DIAMOND

A wife should be beautiful on the inside as well as the outside

1 Peter 3:3-4, "Don't be concerned about the outward beauty of fancy hairstyles, expensive jewelry, or beautiful clothe. You should clothe yourselves instead with the beauty that comes from within, the unfading beauty and quiet spirit which is so precious to God." (NIV)

This scripture shows God's specific mold for the kind of woman He wants you to be. A wife must take pride in her outward appearance. It is vital for a wife to consider her personal appearance, a very important part of her life. The Bible says that our bodies are the temple of the Holy Spirit. Therefore it must be treated as such. She must be aware of how she dresses, with modesty, being careful not to wear revealing garments that will give others the wrong impression of the woman of God she is. It is very important that a woman consider her body type when she is choosing the clothes she wears. Some women are more blessed than others on the top part of their bodies and some women are more blessed on the bottom part of their bodies. In either, case she has to be very careful not to wear clothes that accentuate that part of her body.

She must also be aware of the amount of make-up she wears. Some of us need more make up than others, but sometimes less make up makes us look better than too much make-up. A wife should make sure her hair looks good, is clean, with a pleasant fragrance. Have you ever hugged a woman and noticed that distinct smell of hair that hasn't been washed for a few days? That is the most disgusting smell. A wife's number one priority should be her personal hygiene which including bathing daily, using under arm deodorant, lotion for her skin, keeping up with her finger nail treatment and pedicure. A husband can feel proud to show her off anywhere; when he knows she takes good care of herself. She must also be aware of the jewelry or accessories she wears. Jewelry should not overpower her overall look.

When we women leave the house, we glance in the mirror at least six times. When we sit in the car, the first thing we do is open the visor mirror, and check our make-up and hair one more time. We make sure everything is in place and we look good. That is perfectly alright but to God the most important thing is the beauty of the heart-- that gentle and quiet spirit that is so precious in God's eyes. A beautiful woman wearing perfect clothing, make-up, shoes, and accessories will appear very unattractive if she speaks in a loud voice, has a bad attitude, is negative and her overall conduct is distasteful. That type of women will bring shame to her husband and may eventually be disliked by others. As Christian women we represent God in all of our ways. A woman with a positive attitude, noble character and a beautiful outside appearance is the perfect combination for the woman who is pleasing to God and brings glory to her husband.

CHARACTERISTICS OF AN "UNPLEASANT WOMAN" (ACROSTIC)

Undermines her husband in public

Negative attitude is her way of life

Pretends to be better than her husband or others

Laughs at her husband's flaws, habits and idiosyncrasies

Enjoys being the center of attraction in a group

Allows herself to be obnoxious and annoying

Settles for what is wrong to say and not for what is best to say in a conversation

Appears to enjoy if a man takes a second look at her physical appearance

Nothing satisfies her more than speaking in a loud voice

Time spent in prayer it is not on her daily schedule

Words that edify others are not part of her vocabulary

Obviously studying the word of God is not part of her daily routine

Making degrading remarks about others is her way of entertaining people

Advice is not something she is open for

Never recognizes her faults nor gives way to better herself

11

DIAMOND

A wife must be an understanding daughter-in-law

A good wife must gain and maintain a good relationship with her mother-in-law even before she says, I do. I have heard people saying, if a man is a good son, he will be a good husband. So if your husband has had a good relationship with his mother, I can assure you, he will be a wonderful husband. On the other hand, he expects you to love and respect his parents just as much as he does. Sometimes it is hard to accomplish certain goals in your relationship with the in-laws when the mother-in-law is one of those who has spoiled her son throughout his life; keep in mind everything can be accomplished as we place our relationship in the hands of God. A good mother is very protective with her children and she will defend them above anything or anybody.

I had a wonderful mother-in-law but I only had the opportunity to interact with her for two years. We moved away from her very early in our marriage, but I saved in my heart, the most wonderful memories of my time with her. She, like any other mother, loved her son but she showed me the same love and respect. She always made me feels very much a part of her life and family. She taught me, in such a loving way, my husband's likes and dislikes, especially with food, in the way he likes certain things. I was able to understand my husband better once I decided to become close to her and I began to call her mama just like my husband did. She was actually his grandmother and she had raised him and his two sisters from the time he was a year old. I connected with her as soon as I was able to show her how much I loved her son and how much I wanted to learn everything I could to please him. She loved her son but never was over protective and treated us the same. My mother also, from day one, loved him just like she loved me. Needless to say, I had two wonderful examples to follow.

I believe my situation was very unique. I realize that there are many women who have a good relationship with their mother-in-law. As godly women, we need to consider the position of our mother-in-law. She raised this man from childhood to manhood and did the best she could, sometimes with very few resources. Then you came into his life, and she felt as if another woman had replaced her. So she had to adjust to that fact, which was very difficult.

Other women do not have a good relationship with their mother but her husband has always had a good relationship with his mother. In that case, it is difficult for the wife to understand why her mother-in-law is so close to her son.

This can also happen with brothers and sisters-in-law. After my husband and I had been married for about four years, my sister-in-law came to visit for a while and the second day she was with us, she got up early in the morning and made us breakfast. She and my husband were in the kitchen having a good time talking, laughing and reminiscing about old times. They hadn't seen each other for a few years. She served the kids and proceeded to serve my husband. I had been observing what was going on in the kitchen from afar and I was feeling a little jealous because I had never experienced that kind of relationship with my own brother. I couldn't understand their closeness and the things they had shared as children. When I saw that, I immediately went up to her and told her, "he is my husband and I serve him his food." You can imagine the rest. It was a very awkward and uncomfortable situation for her and my husband. She didn't know what to say. She hadn't done anything wrong and my husband felt trapped between her and I. That was a very childish comment on my part. I made her feel really bad, but I was young, inexperienced, and I didn't realize the mistake I had made. Years later I was able to apologize to her and explain how jealous I was of their beautiful brother/sister relationship. From that moment on, I committed myself to teach my children how to treat each other and their future in-laws. My sister-in-law and I now have a wonderful relationship and I love her as if she is my real sister.

I encourage you to do your best to begin your marriage by trying to develop a good relationship with your future mother-in-law. Some can be very difficult to deal with, but I believe that if you try to become her friend, even before you marry her son, you may win her over sooner than you think. Call her every once in a while, invite her out to lunch, send her flowers for no reason and remember her birthday. Begin to pick her brain about her son and tell her how fascinated you are about becoming the women her son needs for a wife. Show interest in knowing more about his likes and dislikes. Do not overdo it by selling yourself too high above her expectations. Remember, some mothers think there is no woman good enough for their son. Be sincere, humble and cordial with her; treat her with respect, letting her know how good of a job you think she did as a mother raising such a wonderful man. She will begin to trust you with her son's future with no regrets.

THE HOUSEWIFE

12

DIAMOND

A housewife must know how to Cook

"**A way to a man's heart is through his stomach.**" I'm sure you have heard this many times. Many young women are going into marriage with no knowledge of the culinary art. They figure TV dinners are pretty good, they know how to make a sandwich, or they can always stop at the market and pick up a roasted chicken. This is OK every once in a while, but your husband can't live on TV dinners or precooked meals forever. Some young brides don't even know how to make hard-boiled eggs, literally. I asked this question to a young lady. I said, "Do you know how to cook?

She said, "No."

I said. "Can you make hard boiled eggs"?

She said, No, How do you do that?"

Unbelievable but true. I have talked to young married women who were very frustrated not knowing how to put a meal together. If you are one of those young women, I suggest you begin preparing yourself for this aspect of marriage. It is as important as any other area in your marriage. People say that you win a man over with food. It is not so for every man, because there are men who are better in the kitchen than some woman. Even then, every man prefers to come home from a hard day at work and find his wife with dinner ready for him. There are many simple and delicious meals you can prepare that will satisfy your husband's taste.

We live in a fast life society where many wives find themselves having to help their husbands in the work force. Therefore many mothers are not taking the time to instruct their young daughters in the preparation of meals. I have dedicated this section of my book to help you acquire basic skills that will help you be successful in the kitchen. The first thing you need to do is find out what your husband's likes and dislikes are when it comes to food, if you don't already know. What kind of man is he? Is he a rice and beans man, a meat and potato man, or a pasta man"? Is he a fan of Mexican food, American food, or food from his country? Then begin to find ways in which you can be creative with his favorite foods. For example, if he is a rice and beans man you need to find ways to make rice and/or beans in different ways to make it satisfying for him and at the same time easy for you to make while you are learning. If he is a meat and potato man, then find different ways to make potatoes. They can be served with different types of meat and so on.

There are many ways to make a variety of meals that are simple, fast and easy to make. I was born and raised in Puerto Rico and our meals always included rice, so my mother found different ways to make rice. Like rice with chicken, rice with beans, rice with shrimps, rice with sausage, rice with corn, and so on. I suggest that after finding out your husband's favorite meals; you begin to combine ingredients to prepare a variety of meals according to his taste, his likes, and dislikes.

I have compiled a group of recipes, some simple to make with simple ingredients that you will be able to prepare in a short period of time. Some are more elaborate to help you with special day meals.

13
DIAMOND

A housewife must take good care of her home

A one carat ruby is worth twice as much as a one carat diamond! In the book of **Proverbs 31:10-31,** it speaks about, "a wife of noble character." The writer describes a wife of noble character as a woman more valuable than rubies. For a man, a valuable wife is one who is totally dedicated to please God first of all, then dedicated to please him. You need to be a woman who is able and willing to take care of the affairs of his home. She makes sure the house is clean, laundry is done, meals are made on time, and in some cases, the finances of the home are well managed. You may think I am going to teach you how to scrub the floors, clean the restroom and dust the furniture. Well no, I don't want to dwell on the "how to," but the consistency of it. Most of us are busy women; many of us are in ministry and so I understand the struggles of a woman who is a wife, a mother and is in ministry. You may be a young girl barely getting ready to become a wife or maybe you just got married, in either case, you will find that "marriage and family" can become a little overwhelming if you are a working wife. If you make a decision, early in your marriage, to keep your household in order, it will never be overwhelming. It will become a good habit. I realize it does get tiring at times, but if you learn to make a schedule for yourself, it will not overwhelm you. I know many women who have raised three, or more children being in the ministry and having full time jobs and have been able to manage keeping their house in order by keeping a schedule. If you are a working wife who has a ministry you must live on a schedule. Let me help you with that. When my husband and I got married I had a full time job. I had a honeymoon baby, so for the first 10 months of our marriage I was dealing with hormones, throwing up, swollen hands and feet and weak bladder and trying to make my husband understand that he was supposed to satisfy every craving. Also trying to cope with the extra 45 pounds I gained in 9 months. On top of that, I was expected to get up early in the morning to make breakfast and a sack lunch, bend over to clean behind the toilet, stretch out to clean the shower and tub, sweep and mop the whole house, dust the furniture, remember to take meat out of the freezer in preparation for dinner, and have dinner on the table when he walked in tired from work. At the end of my pregnancy, I could hardly walk but still felt like I needed to do all those things every day in order to keep my husband happy and my house clean.

That wasn't easy to do, but I learned later in my life that all those things had to be done but with a weekly schedule it would have worked better and with less stress. So I came up with a schedule that gave me less to do and more "me time." I divided all my chores through the week. I started by including the everyday things we have to do like cooking, making the bed, attending to my husbands and keeping the kitchen clean etc. and added one more chore to every day. For example Monday: double scrub the kitchen, Tuesday: double scrub the bathroom, Wednesday: do the laundry, Thursday: dust, vacuum and mop, Friday: do errands, go to the market etc. You can change it as it seems more convenient to you. A word of advice: try to do your chores in the morning hours when the temperature is cooler. If you are a working wife try to do some in the morning some at night to alleviate the load. The main thing is that you keep up with the cleaning so it doesn't become a big load, all at once. The Word of God says in ***Philippians 4:13 "For I can do all things through him who gives me strength." (NIV)*** If you have the strength that only God can give and a good weekly schedule to follow, I assure you, you will have more time to enjoy with your husband and children and more "me time."

THE MOTHER,
MOTHER-IN-LAW
AND
GRANDMOTHER

DIAMOND

A Good Mother is dedicated to her children

I n this modern world there are many different opinions on how to raise a child. They have many forms of discipline and many laws that protect the children, but there are more child abuse cases reported today than ever before. Thousands of children are reported as abused and neglected every year, not counting those not reported. Over the years, more than 20,000 American children are believed to have been killed in their own homes by family members. In the year 2014 it was said that 1,825 children were abused or neglected each day in the U.S. Statistics say: Nationwide, more than 463,000 children live in foster care. In California, which has the largest foster care population than any other state, the number of fostered youth has tripled in the last 20 years. 18% of children in foster care are there due to physical abuse in their homes, 65% emancipate from the foster care without a place to live, 40% of people living in homeless shelters are former foster children, less than 3% go to college. Statistics can be depressing, but the individual painful and unbearable stories associated with these statistics demand both action and hope.

What can we do to prevent our children from becoming part of a statistic? Raising a child is not the easiest task, especially in this time and age. **Proverbs 22:6 (AMP), "*Train up a child in the way he should go and even when he is old, he will not depart from it.*" (NIV)** In order for us to train up a child in the way he should go, we need to learn some very simple principles. It is wise to take a look at your childhood from time to time for positive ways of disciplining that you may have experienced in your growing up years. Things you remember your parents doing that had an impact on your behavior. No parent is perfect, we have all made mistakes in our effort to train our children in a godly way. Some parents have done the best they could with the resources they had to discipline and care for their children. I was raised in a Christian home, very sheltered and limited on things I was allowed to do. I thank God for my parents and the upbringing techniques they used to raise me, even though many times, I didn't agree with their decisions.

As I look back at my childhood, I realize how much of an impact their way of disciplining had on my life as an adult. I was the younger of two children and the only girl. My brother is seven years older than me, so in reality, I was the spoiled baby, especially by my father. So, at times, they didn't agree with each other concerning our discipline. The one thing they both agreed on was **instilling the love and the fear of God in our hearts**. I learned very early in my childhood to love Jesus and to try to do everything he wanted me to do. On the other hand, my husband was raised in a very loving but liberal home where religion was not one of the strongest points and the liberty to do ungodly things was ramped. We tried to use some of my parent's ways of raising us, with our children. As I have mentioned, no parent is perfect so needless to say, we have some regrets. I say this because I don't want you to feel like a failure as a parent. You have to maintain a strong relationship with God and your husband to be the best parent you can be. Parenthood is for both mom and dad, so before you make any decision for your children, you have to speak with your spouse and come to an agreement concerning any decision on disciplinary actions.

Every child is different, they all have their individual character and ways to respond to different situations. We have to know how to handle each child according to who they are without showing any preference. For example, generally, boys are tough and girls are gentle, so we should respect their needs and differences as we discipline. There will be times when one needs more attention than the other and we should give them the attention.

Parenting requires sacrifice, but it is the most rewarding sacrifice in the world. Parenting requires total dedication, but it is the most gratifying experience a parent can have. Sacrificing your time and effort for your children will show them your love and dedication to their well being. Always think of things you wanted your parents to do for you. This will give you an idea of what they expect from you. It is always wise to spend quality time with each child individually. Go out for a bite to eat with them, this makes them feel important and special. Ask them what they expect from you as a parent and allow them to express themselves without interrupting them. This teaches them to respect others when they are talking. Obeying traffic laws and being polite to police officers will teach a child how to have respect for the law and authority.

The following are some tips that can help you make

decisions according to the situation at hand, and/or help you prevent situations that are at times, hard to handle.

1. **Be his or her friend** - Remember that you are not only an authority figure, but also a friendly face for the child to communicate with. Think of your friends, the ones you can fully rely on to share your secrets and deepest feelings. That is what they need. Don't use the secrets they tell you to formulate future punishments, gifts, fun days or trips. Never expose to others their secrets, desires and feelings that they have shared in private. And most of all, keep your promise to keep what they tell you a secret.

2. **Be a good example to your children** - "Monkey-see monkey-do," is a very common and true statement. If you want your child to grow up to be a man or woman of integrity, have good morals and be compassionate with others, then *you* need to be that model. Children learn more by example than they do by books, lectures, or any other way of instruction. There is a good chance your children will repeat what they see you do. Always try to be the person you want your children to be. It doesn't mean you have to be perfect or that you can't show your weaknesses. Children should learn how to work with or around shortcomings and problems. If you can, apologize when you're wrong to your child as well as in front of your child. This will make a far greater impact than if you never admit your mistakes. One of the biggest life lessons a parent can give a child is that it's okay to be wrong and apologize.

3. **Try to relate with your children** - Relating to certain situations will allow your child to feel as if you understand them. Sharing a similar story that

happened in your own life, perhaps as a child or as an adult, the child will then be more open with you.

4. **Honesty is of utmost importance** - Children in general, not only troubled children, are very good at detecting dishonesty because, more than likely, they have been lied to in the past. If you cannot relate to the child, do not pretend that you can, because the child will know that you are lying. Being dishonest will make it harder for the child to trust and open up to you and others.

5. **Your child needs someone who will listen** - Why not you? The most significant thing a child needs is someone who pays attention and listens to what they have to say. Some troubled children do not have anyone in their life that cares enough to listen to them. Parenting a child is not always sharing your knowledge or thoughts, but allowing the child to share their life with you.

6. **Make time to plan for the future with your child** - Part of parenting is making simple long or short-term goals for the child to accomplish. The sense of accomplishment is something every child needs; therefore, you need to help pave the way for the child's success. It is more powerful if you allow them to set their own goals. Listen to their individual goals and help them refine their goal setting. Discuss their goals with them and set it up so the child feels good about making decisions after looking at all the alternatives. The achievement of those goals becomes more important to their confidence in life when they are responsible for reaching the goals.

Encourage long term goals like their future career or something they would like to do when they grow older. If, for example, a child would like to own a horse someday, they can become knowledgeable about the care of horses. A trip to the country side where there are horses and other farm animals will encourage the child to become a farm owner one day. If they are fascinated by music, cooking, medicine or whatever it is- one day they might end up being a famous musician, singer, chef or a doctor. People are happiest in life if they love their work.

7. **Make fun days a vital part of your family life** - Remember that the child you are raising is still a kid and wants to have fun. Allowing the child to forget their past or present problems and act their age is something they will thrive on. This will also relax the child and make them feel like they can trust you and open up to you because they consider you to be *a friend*.

8. **Embrace your child daily** - Above all things, your child needs to know and feel loved by you more than anyone else in his/her life. Let them know they are loved unconditionally. Remember how God loves us. Whether your child behaves or not, they need to know mom and dad will never hold love from them. A big part of their success in life depends on the support they receive from mom and dad, even as adults. Never push your child away when they get close to you looking for affection, no matter how upset you are with them. If they don't get the affection they are looking for in you, they may go find it elsewhere, hopefully not from the wrong person.

9. **Show them to love God above all things** - Showing a child the love and the fear of God is the most important thing the parent can do. Teach them to pray and encourage them to have some time for daily prayer, and it is essential that they see you praying. Have them experience the awe of God in all they see and do.

15
DIAMOND

A Mother must understand her position as a mother-in-Law

Mothers-in-law have had, "a not so great" reputation in this world. They are often thought of as the enemy of the marriage rather than someone who loves her child. I agree there are mothers that have not learned to win over their sons or daughters-in-law. The only way to win over your son or daughter-in-law is with love and respect. We need to understand that our children will grow up and become independent. They will meet someone and get married one day. As mothers we need to learn how to accept their decision of beginning a new life as a husband or a wife. Not all mothers in law fully understand their roll and the impact it has on their children. As mothers in law we are called to love and treat our children and their partners with the same respect. They need to know that you approve of the person they chose to be their mate. If you don't agree, you should be able to advise them but they need to make their own decisions in life. The roll of a mother-in-law begins before her child's wedding; it begins when they are dating. The first impression of you is what they will remember forever. Try to make the first impression a positive one. That is where you begin to build a relationship with them. His or her priorities have changed and mom and dad are now priority #2. His or her partner and their children have become priority #1. This may sound harsh and painful but it doesn't have to be, if we as mothers understand our position in the lives of our adult children. Try to remember when you met your mother-in-law and the relationship you have had with her. That will help you be the mother-in-law your children desire. The Bible says in **Mark 10:7-8,** *"For this reason a man will leave his father and mother and be united to his wife and the two will become one flesh.* **(NIV)** This Bible verse is not only for us to understand the law of husband and wife as becoming one flesh, but it also means that parents ought to understand and recognize their position as in laws." We will forever be mom and dad but our responsibilities, at some point, shift a little and it takes time to adjust to our position. It is time for them to begin to make their own decisions. From time to time they will need our advice and if they ask, we will gladly give it, but the decisions are for them to make.

After my youngest son got married they had the need to live with us for a while and during that time I began to realize how important it was for my son to know that I was happy about the decisions they were making. One specific time he asked me what my opinion was about a certain decision he had to make and this was my answer, "This is my opinion, but if you have to make a decision between my opinion and your wife's opinion, please take hers. Never choose mom's advice over your wife's advice. I would be very hurt if your dad thought that your grandma's opinion was more important to him that mine." I also said, "Be very careful how you approach this situation. I am older and have more life experience but she is your wife and deserves all your consideration and respect regarding any decision you have to make. Make sure you sit with her and figure out this situation together. Consider your dad's and my opinion but never mention our opinion as being better than hers. She is your wife and deserves your respect. Mom and dad will always be here to help you with anything you need, but you need to respect her and work things out with her first. This is what keeps peace in the home." I believe I have a good relationship with my daughter-in-law because I learned to respect her opinion, no matter what, by instilling in my son respect toward his wife.

So the bottom line is, learn to love and respect your daughters and sons-in-law early in their relationship. They may not understand everything, but your love and respect for them will teach them how to respect you as a mother and friend rather than a mother-in-law.

My mother loved my husband from the minute she met him. I could never go to my mother complaining in any way about my husband. She would always send me back saying, "you must learn to give your husband his place as the man of the house and sit and discuss all matters with him. You need to pray together and ask God to help you make the right decisions." She continued the conversation by saying, "he is a good husband, he loves and respects you. Are you being the wife he wants you to be? If not, you need to reflect on what you are doing and stop coming to me with complaints about him."

They were harsh words coming from a mother to her daughter, but it taught me a lot. It helped me realize how much she respected my husband and, even though, it hurt to see her taking his side rather than mine. It felt good to know she agreed with my decision to marry him. When my mother passed away, her last words were an expression of love toward my husband and I. That was a lesson I have never forgotten. I know not all stories are as good as this one, you may not have had a good relationship with your mother-in-law, but you can change your story by learning how to be a good mother in law to your child's partner. They will appreciate it. Be your daughter-in-law's friend, spend quality time with her, take her shopping and pray for her and with her. Your son will love that about you. Befriend your son-in-law, show him respect and the love of God above all things, even when you don't agree with his ways. That will build a relationship with him that your daughter will love and appreciate.

16
DIAMOND

A mother must be a devoted Grandmother

"**M**others love and teach but Grandmothers teach love.**"** These words were written on a decorative pillow my first granddaughter gave me when she was little. " I really didn't understand what that meant, but as she got older I began to realize that our job as grandmothers is to teach them how to love by the way we love them. Grandmother's love is different than a mother's love and unless you are a grandma you won't understand it. It is an endless love with no comparison except the love of God. We don't love our grandchildren more than we love our children, but it is a deeper love and it is hard to explain. My granddaughters can do no wrong. I defend them over anything or anybody and sometimes as grandmothers we tent to overdo it. But by the time we become grandmothers we are mature and have lived long enough to see and realize the mistakes we made with our children and we are ready to make up for that.

A very wise woman whom I love and respect with all my heart, told me one day, "You don't know what it is to be a woman until you become a grandmother". I had just learned I was going to be grandma for the first time and that really caught my attention. The day I got the call that I was going to be grandma, I was in my office at work and all of a sudden I just started yelling and screaming from the top of my lungs. It was the most wonderful news I had ever heard and it has been the most wonderful journey. I now have 3 gorgeous granddaughters. Loving and caring for these little babies, who are blood of our blood and flesh of our flesh, has been the greatest gift of all. I desire to see my granddaughters daily. When they call me I drop what I'm doing to hear their voices. I want them to know grandma is there for them any time of the day. You see, when we are young raising our children, we become overwhelmed making sure their needs are met. As grandmothers we just have to love because mom and dad are doing the job of making sure their needs are met. No longer do we have to get caught up with the everyday life affairs, all we have to do is love, love, love. My husband and I make sure we are there for every school event, Christmas play, recitals, games, competitions, grandparent's day, and so on. They loved to go to grandma's house overnight because we did fun things with them. We baked cookies, cup cakes, brownies and also made tents in the living room with sheets and had marshmallows fight. Those are memories they will never forget.

But the most important thing we have done is to instill in them the love and fear of God. We used to pick them up to spend the night on Saturdays so they could go to church with us on Sunday morning for Sunday school. They were involved in Christmas plays and children's choir for different occasions. The spiritual part of our family should be the number one item on our prayer list. Teach them, guide them, but most of all pray for them daily, these things will never be forgotten.

Some of us mothers and grandmothers have tried so hard to instill the love and the fear of God into our children and still we are yet to see our children giving their hearts completely to the Lord, but we have to continue to be godly examples for them to follow. The legacy that started with my grandparents continued with my parents and will continue to our children's children *2 Timothy 1:5, " I am reminded of your sincere faith, which first lived in your grandmother Lois and in your mother Eunice and, I am persuaded, now lives in you also." (NIV)* Teach them not only to love God, but to honor Him and have faith in Him for everything they need. As they see you trusting and believing, they will also begin to trust and believe. My youngest son moved miles away with his wife and my two younger granddaughters. To this day I receive late night phone calls from my granddaughters when they can't sleep or when they have things on their minds that they are not able to sort through. They say, "Gradma can you pray for me", and my heart rejoices in the fact that they recognize that there is someone who cares and can help them in their time of need. I pray for them daily, but when they ask for prayer it is my highest honor to pray for them. I know as they get older, they will always remember grandma's love for God and for them.

EPILOGUE

As we come to the end of this book, I pray you have been able to learn and value each diamond just as you will the diamond that sits or will be sitting on your finger. Nothing makes a man happier than to know that his bride takes time to educate herself with facts that will enhance their relationship. God has a plan for your marriage and the only way that plan can come to pass is by:

1. **Having an intimate relationship with God daily.**

Pouring your heart out to God in prayer brings about the peace and assurance that whatever you encounter will be in the plan of God for your marriage.

2. **Putting into practice everything you have learned.**

Regular exercise of an activity or skill is the way to become proficient in it. In other words, you become better at whatever you do if you do it often. You will never be a perfect wife, but you will get better at it if you practice it daily

3. **Paying very close attention to every need your husband may have.**

Be his friend and allow him to be able to consider you his confidant by listening to his heart and not only what he has to say.

4. **Praying with your husband daily.**

Be his prayer partner by being by his side during his prayer time. Let him feel like the person you want him to make you feel.

> *"Three things will last forever – faith, hope and love – and the greatest of this is Love"*
> *1 Corinthians 13:13*

RECIPES

The following recipes have been in my kitchen for quite a few years. Some were passed down to me from my mother and grandmother and they continue to be a hit on our table. Some I have taken from my friends and have somewhat altered them or given them a Latin twist to satisfy my family's palate. As you begin your journey in the kitchen, you will find yourself changing the ingredients and the method of making some meals to make it easier or to change the taste according to your family's likes and dislikes. For example, some people do not like sea food, so instead of using tuna in a casserole you may replace it with chicken. You will have to be creative and also innovative in order to be successful in the kitchen. I enjoy cooking; it is my favorite thing to do around the house. So, through the years, I have learned to be creative by changing and replacing ingredients and also putting two, three or four ingredients together to make a meal of my own creation. I encourage you to feel free to change these recipes as you please. You might make some mistakes in the beginning, but that is how we all learn, by making mistakes. Don't give up, try it again, and again until you reach your perfection.

I have also prepared some menus that will help you plan your meals and will help organize your shopping list for the market. In preparing your meals, always remember all meals should include meat or some kind of protein, a vegetable and a starch (pasta, rice, potato or bread).

Sample of dinners for a week (see all the main dish recipes below)

Day 1 - **Meatloaf**, mashed potato, vegetables and/or a salad
Day 2 - **Oven fried chicken**, macaroni and cheese, vegetable and/or a salad
Day 3 - **Pot roast**, white rice
Day 4 – **Spaghetti**, bread and salad
Day 5 - **Chicken enchiladas**, rice and beans
Day 6 - **Mahi Mahi Fish** or any kind of fish, rice pilaf and asparagus or any vegetable
Day 7 - **Time to go out to eat**

QUICK FIX FOR COMMON COOKING MISTAKES

1. ***If your meal is too salty*** try adding something sweet like sugar, honey, brown sugar.
2. ***If you meal is too spicy*** a squeeze of lemon or lime juice can help temper the heat. If the dish calls for any cream or if adding cream is appropriate, you can add heavy cream, milk, coconut milk or sour cream. You can always add a little sugar, brown sugar or honey to balance out the spice.
3. ***If your meal is too sweet*** I try adding a bit of acid or spice. Great flavor is usually a balance of sweet, sour, salty, bitter and spicy. Tinkering with those other elements will help balance anything that's too sweet. It's the reason why

chocolate chip cookies taste so great with just a pinch of salt.

4. *If the sauce or gravy is too watery* I usually use 1 to 2 tablespoons of flour or cornstarch and 1 to 2 tablespoons of water or the sauce or gravy. Dissolve the flour or cornstarch with the liquid, and stir it into the dish to help thicken it a bit.

5. *If the meat is overcooked* is normally tough and hard to chew, I usually will slice it thin and serve it with a sauce or a gravy or shred it and make another recipe.

6. *If your vegetables (like broccoli) are overcooked* dice or chop them to toss in pasta or rice. Or you could toss them in breadcrumbs and place in a baking dish with some light cream or half-and-half, cheese and herbs and make a casserole.

Here are some tips to help you avoid certain cooking mistakes:

1. *When cooking pasta* make sure there is plenty of water in the pot and let the water come to a boil before adding the pasta, add plenty of salt and a little bit of oil to keep the pasta from becoming sticky. Also if you are not serving the pasta immediately after is cooked, drained all the water out and add a little bit of oil or butter, stir it well and set aside until you are ready to add any sauce.

2. *When cooking pork chops* make sure the frying pan is very hot, lower the fire and place the pork chops on the pan, do not turn over until the bottom sides is light brown, otherwise you will end up with a tough piece of meat. You can bake them instead.

3. ***When cooking chicken*** make sure you wash your hands right after handling it and do not taste the seasoning after is on the chicken.

4. ***When meat is hot***, the muscle fibers contract and disperse juice. If you cut into it right away, the juices wind up on the cutting board instead of inside the meat, steaks, chicken etc. To avoid that from happening let the meat rest for about 5-10 minutes after cooking so the muscles can relax and the juices redistribute (make a tent with foil and place on top of the meat to prevent it from losing too much heat.

5. ***When baking a cake*** from a box to avoid a dry cake add a little more oil than required on the instruction, you will end up with a soft and moist cake.

6. ***When cooking a steak*** heat a frying pan on high flame then add the steak and lower the flame a medium to low flame to avoid a chard piece of meat that is raw inside; unless you like it rare or medium rare.

MAIN DISHES

Chicken Fried Steak with Gravy

Ingredients

2 large eggs
1 cup all-purpose flour
2 teaspoons seasoned salt
black pepper
3 thin steaks (beef, veal or chicken)
1 teaspoon salt to taste the flour
½ cup vegetable oil
1 tablespoon butter
1 ½ cups bread crumbs

Gravy:

1/3 cup all-purpose flour
3 cups milk
½ teaspoon seasoned salt or/beef or chicken bouillon
4 tablespoons of butter

Directions for the steaks

For the steak: Begin with setting up an assembly line of dishes.

First Dish, beaten the eggs.

Second Dish, flour mixed with the seasoned salt, 1 ½ teaspoons black pepper.

Third Dish, the bread crumbs.

Then have one clean plate at the end of the line to receive the breaded meat. Work with one piece of meat at a time. Sprinkle both sides with any seasoning you have in your pantry and black pepper, then place it in the (1) **flour mixture**. Turn to coat. Place the meat into the (2) **egg mixture**, turning to coat. Finally, place it on the (3) **bread crumbs** and turn to coat and press the steak with your finger firmly against the dish. It should be (dry mixture/wet mixture/dry mixture). Place the breaded meat on the clean plate, then repeat with the remaining meat.

Heat the oil in a large skillet over medium heat. Add the butter. Cook the meat, until the edges start to look golden brown, about 2 minutes each side. Remove the meat to a paper towel-lined plate and keep them warm by covering lightly with another plate or a sheet of foil. Repeat until all the meat is cooked.

For the gravy: After all the meat is fried, pour out the grease into a heatproof bowl. Without cleaning the skillet, return it to the stove over medium-low heat. Add 4 tablespoons of butter. Once the butter is hot, sprinkle the flour evenly over the butter. Using a whisk, mix the flour with the butter, creating a golden-brown paste. Add more flour if it looks overly greasy; add a little of grease if it becomes too clumpy. Keep cooking until the mixture reaches a deep golden brown color. Pour in the milk, whisking constantly. Add the seasoned salt, and /or chicken bouillon to taste and cook, whisking until the gravy is smooth and thick, 5 to 10 minutes. Be prepared to add more milk if it becomes overly thick. Be sure to taste to make sure gravy is sufficiently seasoned.

Serve the meat next to a side of mashed potatoes.
Pour gravy over the meat and the potatoes
and serve with your favorite vegetable.

Oven Fried Chicken (serves 2)

Ingredients

4 pieces of chicken
2 teaspoons garlic Seasoning (or any seasoning of your choice)
Black pepper
1 teaspoon olive oil

Directions

Mix the garlic seasoning, black pepper and olive oil. Marinate the chicken and place it in a baking dish, bake at 350 for 1 ½ hours. The chicken will taste better if you marinate it the day before; place it in a plastic bag and leave it in the refrigerator over-night.

Oven BBQ chicken (serves 4)

Favorite of my kids

Ingredients

8 chicken thighs
3 tablespoons Lawry's garlic salt
1 tablespoon paprika
1 teaspoon black pepper
1 envelope Sazon (optional)

Sauce

2 cups of Ketchup
1 cup of brown sugar
1 tablespoon Worcestershire sauce
1 tablespoon mustard

Directions

Wash the chicken under cold water and patted dry with a paper towel. Place it in a bow ad add the garlic salt, paprika, black pepper and Sazon. Place the chicken in a baking pan and bake for 1 hour at 350 degrees. Mix all the sauce ingredients together and pour half of the sauce over the chicken, cook for another 30 minutes. You could serve it over white rice and corn on the side or you could serve it with any side dish.

Enchiladas (serves 3)

Ingredients

6 corn tortillas
Small can red or green enchilada sauce
(For home made sauce see below)
1 lg. chicken breast or 2 leg and thigh
2 cups shredded shedder, jack or Colby cheese
Salt and pepper
¼ cup green onions chopped (optional)
1 cup black olives chopped (optional)
2 tablespoons chicken flavor bullion
½ cup vegetable oil

Directions

In a sauce pan boil the chicken breast with the chicken flavor bouillon until well cooked, let it cool off and shred in small pieces. In another pan pour the enchilada sauce and heat to boil, set aside. In a small frying pan heat the oil and fry the tortillas for seconds on each side. (optional) Instead of frying just warm up the tortillas. Place the fried or warm tortillas in a plate. On the bottom of a baking sheet pour a small amount of the sauce. Assemble the enchiladas by wetting the tortillas in the sauce then adding pieces of chicken on the center of the tortillas then put some green onions, black olives and the cheese. Roll it up and place on the baking sheet. Repeat that process until all enchiladas are rolled up. Pour as much of remaining sauce and cheese as you want over the enchiladas. Place them in the oven or microwave oven until cheese is melted.

To make your own red enchilada sauce

Add 4- 6 dry chili peppers in a sauce pot, (guajillo chilis are my first choice) in 4 cups of water, add 4 fresh cloves garlic, ½ onions, and boil for 15 minutes. Put everything in the blender, blend it well and put it through a strainer mixing it with a spoon until all the liquid is drained. Place it back on the stove. In a cup pour 2 tablespoons of flour (or cornstarch) and ¼ cup of water and mix well, then slowly add the flour mixture to the sauce to thicken. Season as needed. Chicken bouillon can be used for seasoning.

FISH

Recipe for 4 (mahi-mahi fish is my favorite)

Ingredients

3 tablespoons butter
1 1/2 teaspoons freshly squeezed lemon juice
2 large garlic cloves, finely chopped
1/4 teaspoon salt, plus additional for seasoning
1/4 teaspoon freshly ground black pepper, plus additional for seasoning
1 1/2 tablespoons chopped fresh basil leaves
3 tablespoons olive oil
4 (6 to 8-ounce) mahi mahi fillets, salmon is also a good choice

Directions

Zesty Basil Butter:
Combine the butter, lemon juice, garlic, salt, pepper, and basil in a medium saucepan and cook over low heat, stirring until the butter melts. Cover and keep warm over low heat.

Heat the oil in a large skillet over medium heat. Season the fish with salt and pepper, to taste. Cook the fish for 3 minutes; then turn and cook until just opaque, about 3 to 4 minutes more. Transfer the fillets to individual plates.

Spoon the warm basil butter over the fish and serve.

Meatloaf Cover with Bacon

Ingredients

1 cup milk
6 bread slices (sandwich bread)
2 pounds ground beef
1 teaspoon salt
¼ teaspoon any seasoned salt
4 eggs, beaten
8 to 12 thin bacon slices

Sauce:

6 tablespoons brown sugar
½ cup ketchup
1 teaspoon mustard
Dash or 2 hot sauce (more if you like)
Dash or 2 Worcestershire sauce

Directions

For the meatloaf: Preheat the oven to 350 degrees F.

Pour the milk over the bread and allow it to soak in for several minutes. Place the ground beef, milk-soaked bread, salt and seasoned salt in a large mixing bowl. Pour in the eggs. With clean hands, mix the ingredients until well combined. Form the mixture into a loaf shape on a foil-lined pan. Lay the bacon slices over the top, tucking them underneath the meatloaf to give the meatloaf some support.

Next, make the tomato sauce: Pour the ketchup into a bowl. Add the brown sugar and mustard, and splash in the hot sauce and Worcestershire sauce. Stir the mixture until well combined. Pour one-third of the sauce over the top of the meatloaf.

Bake for 45 minutes, and then pour over another one-third of the remaining tomato sauce over the meatloaf. Bake for an additional 20 to 25 minutes; the meatloaf should be no longer pink in the middle. Allow to sit 10 minutes before serving.

Serve with the remaining sauce on the side as a dipping sauce

Pot Roast

Ingredients

1 small roast beef (around 3 pounds)
2 carrots
2 medium potatoes
2 celery stalks
1 medium onion
4 cloves of garlic
Salt and black pepper
2 tablespoons olive oil
2 bay leaves
1 envelop Lipton Onion Soup

Directions

Chop the garlic real fine, add salt and pepper and spread the mixture all over the meat. In a Dutch oven or a pot big enough for the piece of meat, heat the olive oil and fried the meat in all sides until dark brown. Add the Lipton onion soup, bay leaves and water just enough to cover the meat and let it boil for at least 2 to 3 hours. (or use a crock pot and cook for 6-7 hours) Add the vegetables and continue to cook until the vegetables are tender. If you want to thicken the broth add 2 tablespoon of flour to ½ cup water and mix well then add to the broth stirring constantly. You could serve it with white rice.

Rib eye Steaks for

Ingredients

2 Ribeye steaks
2 tablespoons beef or steaks seasoning
(Or you could minced 3 cloves of garlic with salt and Pepper)
2 teaspoons olive oil
1 teaspoon lemon juice
1 teaspoon butter

Directions

In a small bowl mix seasoning or garlic mixture, the oil and lemon juice. Rub the mixture on both sides of the steaks. On a frying pan melt the butter on a high flame and place the steaks on the pan and let them cook in high flame for a minutes or two on both sides then lower the flame and cook to your desire.

BEANS

There are many kinds of beans (pinto beans, black beans, red kidney beans, garbanzos beans, white beans etc.) and many ways to make them. I have included on this page a few ways in which you can make them.

Fresh Beans

Fresh beans can be cooked in a crock pot or on the stove by cleaning and rinsing 2 or 3 cups of dried beans (soaking in water overnight is recommended but not necessary). Then cook the beans in a medium pot with enough water to cover them plus 2 inches of water above the beans. Then for flavor you can add 2 or 3 pieces of bacon or a ham hog and 1 small onion. Bring to boil then lower the flame and let them boil for 3 or 4 hours, checking occasionally. You could also put them to cook in a crock pot overnight. You can replace these beans with cooked can beans.

Refried Beans

You can use a small amount of the cooked fresh beans to make refried beans for 2 or one small can of beans

In a frying or sauce pan add 2 tablespoons of oil or bacon fat, add whatever amount of beans you desire. Cook them for a few minutes then mash then with a potato smasher. Add Monterey Jack cheese (optional)

Puerto Rican Beans

(We mostly use light large kidney beans, white beans or garbanzos (chickpeas) for this recipe)

Ingredients

2 tablespoons oil, bacon fat or lard
I can 15 oz or 2 cups cooked beans
2 or 3 cloves chopped garlic
1 small onions and 1 small bell pepper
1 tablespoon fresh cilantro
¼ cup cooked smoke ham (you could replace it with 3 slices of bacon)
½ cup tomato sauce
1 envelope Sazon (Goya seasoning)
Salt and pepper to taste

Directions

In a sauce pan add 2 tablespoons of oil, bacon fat or lard, add the ham and cook for 2 minutes on medium flame, add chopped garlic and cook until golden brown, add the onions, bell pepper and cilantro and cook until the onions become translucent. Add tomato sauce and Sazon. Let all ingredients cook together for about 2 minutes, add the beans, salt and pepper to taste and let it boil for approximately 10 to 15 minutes. Serve with rice. This recipe is good for any kind of beans.

*Sazon is a seasoning found in the Hispanic food section of the market.

Chili Beans

Ingredients

1 15 oz can Pinto Beans
1 small can red chili sauce
1 small can dice tomatoes
1 small can tomatoes sauce
1 small can diced green chili
4 slices of bacon cut in small pieces
1 lb ground beef or chicken
3 cloves of minced garlic
1 small diced onion
¼ cup bell peppers
Salt or beef bouillon to taste

Directions

In a medium sauce pot brown the ground beef, drained the grease and add the first 5 ingredients. Let it boil. In the meantime in a frying pan fried the bacon until golden brown and add it to the bean's pot. (Do not discard the bacon fat) In the bacon grease add the garlic and let it cook until it begins to look golden brown, add the onions and bell pepper. Let the mixture cook for about 2 minutes. Then add to the beans and seasoned with salt or beef or chicken bouillon. Boil in a low flame for about 15 minutes and enjoy.

Easy Bean Salad

Ingredients

15 oz can pinto beans
15 oz can black beans
15 oz can green beans
15 oz can corn
1 large onion chopped in small pieces
2 large tomatoes chopped in small pieces
1 large cucumber chopped in small pieces
1 whole bunch of cilantro chopped in small pieces
The juice from 3 or 4 lemons
Salt and pepper to taste

Directions

Drain and rinse all the canned ingredients, place them in a large bowl, add all the chopped vegetables to the bowl. Add the lemon juice, salt and pepper to taste. Mix all ingredients well and place it in the refrigerator for about 10 to 15 minutes. Serve cold with any meal.

RICE

Spanish Rice (Mexican rice) for 2

Ingredients

1 cup of rice
2 tablespoon canola or veg. oil (pork fat tastes better)
½ cup tomato sauce
2 or 3 cloves of garlic finely chopped
½ small onions
1 tablespoon chopped cilantro
1 ½ cups water
2 tablespoons chicken bouillon or more if desire
½ cup frozen mix vegetables or peas and carrots

Directions

In a small pot or frying pan, cook the rice in the oil until it begins to turn golden brown, add the tomato sauce and cook to a minute or so, add the water and the rest of the ingredients, bring to a boil, lower the flame to medium/low and let it cook for approximately 20 minutes.

Rice with chicken (Arroz con Pollo) Puerto Rican style

Ingredients

4 pieces of chicken
4 cups water
Salt and pepper
1 cup of rice
2 tablespoon canola or veg. oil (pork fat taste better)
½ cup tomato sauce
2 or 3 cloves of garlic finely chopped
½ small onions ½ bell pepper
1 tablespoon chopped cilantro
1 ½ cups water
2 tablespoons chicken bouillon or more if desire
1 envelope of Sazon

Directions

In a sauce pan boil the water with the 4 pieces of chicken for about 10 to 15 minutes.

In a sauce pan heat the oil, add the chopped garlic and stir until golden brown, add the onions and bell pepper and cook for a minute or so stirring occasionally, add the tomato sauce and the Sazon and let it cook for another minute or so, add the rice, the chicken and 2 cups of the broth from the chicken and the chicken bouillon and stir well. Bring to a boil and lower the fire to medium/low cover and cook for 20 minutes.

Rice Pilaf

Ingredients

1 cup of rice (Jasmine rice is the best for this recipe)
2 cups water
1 celery stalk chopped
1 lg. carrot chopped
3 green onions chopped
2 cloves of garlic
3 tablespoons chicken bouillon or more if desired
4 tablespoons butter

Directions

In a thick sauce pan or pot melt the butter and add the garlic, cook until golden brown. Add celery, carrots and green onions. Cook for a few minutes add the rice, stir everything together and add the water. Season with chicken bouillon, let it boil then lower the fire and cook for 20 minutes.

White Rice

Serves 2

In a sauce pot boil 1 ½ cups of water, add 2 teaspoons of oil and salt to taste, after the water boils add 1 cup of rice, cover, lower the fire and cook for 20 minutes.

PASTA

Mac and cheese

Ingredients

1 pound bag dried macaroni
4 tablespoons butter
¼ cup all-purpose flour
2 ½ cups whole milk
1 pound sharp Cheddar cheese, plus more for baking
Salt
Seasoned salt
½ teaspoon ground black pepper
Optional spices: cayenne pepper, paprika, thyme

Directions

Preheat the oven to 350 degrees F.

Cook the macaroni until still slightly firm. Drain and set aside. In a large pot, melt the butter and sprinkle in the flour. Whisk together over medium-low heat. Cook for a couple of minutes, whisking constantly. Don't let it burn. Pour in the milk, add the mustard and whisk until smooth. Cook until very thick, about 5 minutes. Reduce the heat to low. Stir until smooth. Add in the cheese and stir to melt. Add ½ teaspoon salt, ½ teaspoon seasoned salt and the pepper. Add any additional spices if desired. Taste the sauce and add more salt and seasoned salt as needed! DO NOT UNDERSALT.

Pour in the drained, cooked macaroni and stir to combine. Serve immediately (while it's still very creamy) or pour into a buttered baking dish, top with extra cheese and bake until bubbly and golden on top, 15 to 20 minutes.

Options: Open a box of instant Mac and Cheese and follow the directions in the box instead.

Pasta and Broccoli Casserole

Ingredients

2 pounds elbow macaroni or any pasta
1 can cream of chicken soup
1 can cream of celery soup
1 cup celery chopped
½ cup green onions
1 small bag frozen broccoli or 2 cups fresh broccoli
2 cups mozzarella cheese
Salt and pepper

Directions

Cook the pasta according to directions in the bag. Drain and add the cream of chicken and cream of celery, celery, onions, frozen broccoli, salt and pepper, mix well. Pour all the ingredients in a baking dish and add the cheese over it. Cover with foil and cook in a 350 oven for 30-45 minutes.

MEATBALLS

For Spaghetti or Sandwiches

Ingredients

1 pound ground turkey or beef
1 pound ground chicken
1 large egg
1/3 cup bread crumbs
¼ teaspoon Italian seasoning
¼ teaspoon each salt and black pepper
2 tablespoon olive oil

Directions

Combine ground turkey and chicken, egg, bread crumbs, Italian seasoning, salt and black pepper. Gently mix all ingredients together with your hands. Form the meatballs wetting your hands occasionally. Bake the meatballs at 350 for 45 minutes or until done. You could add any spaghetti sauce to the meatballs and serve over pasta or make sandwiches with mozzarella cheese.

SOUPS

Tuscan Soup

Ingredients:
Serves 4

1 lb mild Italian sausage chopped in small pieces
2 large russet potatoes, sliced in half, and then in thin slices
1 large onion, chopped
3 or 4 slices of bacon (chopped and cook)
3 garlic cloves, minced
2 cups kale chopped
3 quart water
1 cup heavy whipping cream
chicken bouillon to your taste

Directions:

Cook the chopped bacon until golden brown in a soup pot and remove it from the pot Add the chopped sausages and Brown sausage in a soup pot. Add chicken bouillon and water to pot and stir. Place onions, potatoes, and garlic in the pot. Cook on medium heat until potatoes are done. Add bacon and salt and pepper to taste. Simmer for another 10 minutes. Turn to low heat. Add kale and cream. Heat through and serve. If you want remove the bacon before serving.

Meatball Soup

Ingredients

6 cups of water
1 lb ground beef
¼ cup uncooked rice
2 tbls garlic salt
1 tbls chopped cilantro
1 egg
¼ cuo of chopped onion
3 chopped cloves of garlic
1 tbls of vegetable or olive oil
1 lg potatoe
2 carrots
1 lg Corn on a cob cut in 4 pieces
1 zucchini
1 cup of
Chicken or beef bouillon to your taste

Directions

In a medium pot add the water and begin to boil it. In a big bowl combine the meat, rice, garlic salt, cilantro and the egg. Mix well and made medium size balls (a small ice cream scooper will be helpful to form the balls) Add the meatballs to the boiling water and let them cook for about 10 minutes. While the meatballs are boiling add the oil to a small frying pan then add the onion and garlic and cook for a minute or so then add it to the pot with the meatballs. Chop all the vegetables in medium sizes and add them to the pot. Cook for about 15 to 20 minutes checking every 5 minutes until meat balls are well done.

Turkey and Spinach dish

Ingredients

1 pound ground turkey or chicken
2 0r 3 cups fresh spinach
1 small can diced tomatoes
3 tsp. butter or olive oil
3 cloves of garlic
½ of a small onion chopped
Chicken bouillon to taste

Directions

In a medium frying pan add the butter or olive oil, add the garlic and cook until golden brown. Add the chopped onion and diced tomatoes and cook for 2 minutes, add the ground turkey or chicken and cook it stirring until well done. Add the spinach and let it cook on a low flame for 1 to 2 minutes. Serve over white rice

VEGETABLES

Green Beans and Tomatoes

Ingredients

4 pieces of bacon
1 large onion, chopped
2 pounds fresh green beans, trimmed
Three 14.5-ounce cans whole tomatoes with juice
Salt and black pepper
Cayenne pepper (optional)

Directions

Add the bacon to a large pot and cook over medium heat until light golden (not crisp). Drain off the excess fat, and then add the onions. Cook until the bacon and onions are golden brown. Add the green beans and tomatoes to the pan. Sprinkle in salt, black pepper and cayenne pepper to taste. Stir gently to combine, cover the pot and reduce the heat to low. Simmer for 20 to 30 minutes.

Corn and Zucchini Casserole

Ingredients

Serves 2
1 large zucchini sliced
2 cups can corn
1 small onion chopped
1 medium tomato
2 cloves garlic minced
1 ½ cup Monterey Jack cheese
3 tablespoons butter
Salt and pepper

Directions

In a skillet melt butter and add the garlic, cook for a minute, Add the onion and tomato and cook for 2 minutes, add the zucchini and corn, mix together add salt and pepper to taste. Cover and cook until zucchini is well done. Add the cheese, turn off the fire and cover until the cheese is melt and serve.

Individual Grilled Potatoe Pockets

Ingredients

French Frys Cut Potatoes
Butter
Garlic Salt
Pepper
Individual Aluminum Foil squares (one per person)

Directions

Cut the potatoes in long strips. (Pealing them is optional).
Place as many potatoes strips as you can in the foil square.
Add a small amount of butter over the potatoes and sprinkle
garlic salt and pepper to your liking. Wrap them by folding the
aluminum foil on top of the potatoes leaving some room on
top, and then fold the sides upward to close completely. Place
on the BBQ grilled for about 15 to 20 minutes checking them
every 10 minutes depending on how high the flame is. Serve
with any BBQ meat or chicken.